W9-CQK-660

978   Streeter
Prairie Trails & Cow Towns

$ 5.00 FEE PLUS FULL PRICE FOR EACH ITEM LOST

WILLITS PUBLIC LIBRARY

Please use this book carefully and return it promptly.

Fines are charged for books overdue,
damaged, or lost.

Come often—we like to see you.

Prairie Trails
& Cow Towns

THE DEVIN-ADAIR
ILLUSTRATED WESTERN AMERICANA SERIES

ROY BEAN: *Law West of the Pecos* by C. L. Sonnichsen

I'LL DIE BEFORE I'LL RUN: *The Story of the Great Feuds of Texas* by C. L. Sonnichsen

THE SOUTHWEST IN LIFE & LITERATURE: *An Anthology of Southwestern Writing* edited by C. L. Sonnichsen

TULAROSA: *Last of the Frontier West* by C. L. Sonnichsen

THE OUTLAW TRAIL: *A History of Butch Cassidy and His Wild Bunch* by Charles Kelly

THE CUSTER STORY: *The Life and Intimate Letters of General George A. Custer and His Wife Elizabeth.* Edited by Marguerite Merington

THE ISLANDS AND PORTS OF CALIFORNIA: *A Guide to Coastal California* by Duncan Gleason

I'VE KILLED MEN: *An Epic of Early Arizona* by Jack Ganzhorn

PRAIRIE TRAILS & COW TOWNS: by Floyd Benjamin Streeter

THE PINTO HORSE (fiction): by Charles Elliott Perkins

Prairie Trails & Cow Towns

The Opening of the Old West

FLOYD BENJAMIN STREETER

Illustrated

THE DEVIN ADAIR COMPANY

NEW YORK · 1963

NOTE: This book was originally published in a very small
edition in 1936 in Boston by Chapman & Grimes. The
present edition, reset and printed from new plates,
contains additional photographs and maps.

918

Copyright 1936 by Chapman & Grimes
Copyright © 1963 by The Devin-Adair Company

All rights reserved
No portion of this book may be reproduced in any form
without written permission from the publisher
The Devin-Adair Company
23 East 26th Street, New York 10, N.Y.
except by a reviewer, who may quote brief passages
in connection with a review.
Canadian Agents: Thomas Nelson & Sons, Ltd., Toronto

Printed in the U.S.A.
Library of Congress Catalog Card Number: 63-15595

Preface

For several years, the author has been collecting stories and songs of the Old West. The collection has become quite large and covers a wide range of subjects. Because of the interest in this collection and the demand for the stories, this volume is being published. In view of the fact that it would be impossible to print the entire collection under one cover, it has been decided to issue this volume containing representative tales of the trails, cow towns, and buffalo range, and to publish additional volumes containing other stories at a future date.

The material presented here has been collected chiefly from contemporaneous sources—pioneer newspapers, journals, diaries, scrapbooks, manuscript letters, and state, county, and municipal records, and the reminiscences of eye witnesses. The writer has traveled hundreds of miles, interviewed numerous pioneer settlers, and visited many libraries, archives departments, newspaper offices, county court houses, and city halls in his search for data to make the stories complete and accurate.

A number of difficulties have been encountered. Valuable information is lacking because the records containing the data have been destroyed. In other instances, the records have been located, after a long search, in a dark corner of a stuffy vault, or in a stack of dust-covered documents stored in the attic or basement of a public building. More than one version of some stories and conflicting details in others have necessitated a search for the truth, which search, in several instances, has been fruitless.

It is impossible to acknowledge adequately the debt I owe to those who have aided me so generously in making this collection and in preparing this volume. Acknowledgment is made to members of the faculty and student body of the Fort Hays Kansas State College who have supplied stories and songs and aided in various other ways; to my Uncle, H. W. Prouty; and many others whose names cannot be mentioned because of lack of space. I am indebted to Professor R. R. Macgregor for valuable suggestions on the manuscript. I wish to thank the librarians and newspaper men for the many courtesies extended to me.

F. B. S.

Contents

PREFACE   v

THE WAGON TRAILS   3
Santa Fe and Old Oregon trails. Stage Lines. Hardships.
Pleasures. Indian Attacks. Fight on the Little Blue. Battle
Near Cow Creek. Stage Attacked Near Fort Dodge. Raid
on the Butterfield Line. Indian War in 1868. Storms. Eastern
Notables Drenched. Lost on the Prairie. Horace Greeley's
Overland Journey to California. Ben Holladay's Hold-up.
Record Stage Trips. F. X. Aubry's Record Horseback Rides.
The Pony Express. Freight and Emigrant Trains. Council
Grove. Government Train Attacked at Pond Creek. Mormon
Grove. Counting Stops an Indian Attack. A Shrewd Business
Transaction. A German Farmer's Loss. Snakes. Mirages. The
Caches. Treasure Legend of the Santa Fe Trail. Bullwhackers.
"Our Firm Doesn't Make that Point." A Surprised Tender-
foot.

THE CATTLE TRAILS   53
Establishing the Kansas-Texas Trails. The Northern Drive.
Stampedes. High Water. Indians. Outlaws. Cattleman versus
Farmer.

THE KANSAS COW TOWNS   69
Abilene. Ellsworth. Newton. Wichita. Dodge City.

THE BUFFALO RANGE   167
Vast Herds on the Plains. Buffalo Hunt with the Miamis.
With the Omaha Indians on a Buffalo Hunt. Buffalo Drank

the Solomon River Dry. How William F. Cody Acquired
the Sobriquet "Buffalo Bill." Cody's Defense of His New
Title. Matt Clarkson. Sidelights on the Royal Hunt—Buffalo
Hunt Along the Kansas Pacific. A Buffalo Hunt Near Hays.
Witches on the Plains. Fight with a Buffalo. A Detroiter's
First Hunt. A Day on Big Creek. Storms. The Wild Huntress.
Songs of the Range.

NOTES   199

BIBLIOGRAPHY   205

INDEX   209

ILLUSTRATIONS
Between pages 120-121

Prairie Trails
& Cow Towns

The Wagon Trails

THE trails and stage roads were the overland routes for most of the early western travel. A large portion of the pioneer settlers came west over these routes. The traders, the travelers, the gold diggers, and the soldiers, and before them the Indians, used the trails to reach their destination. These people all had interesting experiences as, day after day, they traveled slowly westward. The stories of what they saw and did make up the literature of the trails and are a part of the pioneer literature of the Old West. Those with poetic ability put their story in verse, and in this way supply us with the songs of the trail. Our purpose in this chapter is to place before the reader representative tales of the leading wagon trails.

Two of these trails, the Sante Fe and the Oregon, are especially fruitful in romance and folk tales. Both trails started at Independence, Missouri. The Santa Fe Trail entered Kansas in what is now Oxford Township, Johnson County, and pursued a course a little south of west to Council Grove. From

3

Council Grove the trail ran in a southwesterly direction, striking the Arkansas River near the site occupied by Great Bend,
and followed the north bank of the river to the present town
of Cimarron in Gray County where it divided; one branch
continued west along the Arkansas, the other crossed the river
and ran southwestward. The Oregon trail entered Kansas
near the mouth of the Kaw River and ran in a westerly direction along the south side of the river to Topeka where the
trail crossed to the north side; it continued west into Potta-
watomi County, turned north into Marshall County, and followed the Big Blue River out of Kansas and the Platte River
valley west through Nebraska.

Stage Lines

Prior to the advent of the railroads west of the Mississippi,
numerous stage lines were established. Some of these ran to
nearby towns; others ran to distant points, such as Denver and
Santa Fe, while the Overland Stage Line ran to California. As
the railroads were built westward, they gradually replaced
the stage lines. Then the stages were used as feeders and to
carry passengers, mail, and express beyond the end of the railroad.

One of the earliest stage routes in the West was over the
Santa Fe Trail, where a monthly line of stages was inaugurated from St. Louis to Santa Fe in 1849. As the line became
more popular the eastern terminus was moved westward to
Independence, Missouri.[1]

A writer in the *Missouri Commonwealth*, published at Independence, July, 1850, described the first stage coaches as
follows:[2] ". . . The stages are got up in elegant style, and are
each arranged to convey eight passengers. The bodies are
beautifully painted, and are made watertight, with a view of

using them as boats in ferrying streams. The team consists of six mules to each coach. The mail is guarded by eight men armed, as follows: Each man has at his side, fastened in the stage, one of Colt's revolving rifles; in a holster below, one of Colt's long revolvers and in his belt a small Colt's revolver, besides a hunting-knife; so that these eight men are ready, in case of attack, to discharge one hundred and thirty-six shots without having to reload . . ."

In a few years, the service was increased to once a week, later to three times a week; in the early sixties daily stages were run from both ends of the route.

The distance from Independence to Santa Fe was about eight hundred miles. It required about two weeks for the stages to make the trip. The baggage allowance for each passenger was limited to forty pounds; all over that amount cost one dollar a pound. The fare included the meals of the travelers, which usually consisted of hardtack, bacon and coffee, and at times an abundance of buffalo and antelope meat.

The Overland Stage route ran in a northwesterly direction from Atchison through Kennekuk and Marysville, crossed the State line into Nebraska near the Little Blue River and continued westward along the Platte River. In 1861 Ben Holladay, a New York capitalist, acquired control of this property and reorganized the company under the name of the "Overland Stage Line." He continued at the head of the firm for five years and built up such a gigantic enterprise that he was known as the "stage king" of America.

The distance from Atchison to Placerville was 1913 miles. The valley of the Platte was a natural highway, a smooth hard stage road having been made by driving over it. Here and there was a gully or a dry creek or petty stream to cross; but, as late as 1865, it was said that there was not a quarter of a mile of bridging between Atchison and Denver. There was an occasional stretch of heavy sand, and some mud after a rain. In good weather, with proper relays and a light load, a speed of ten miles an hour could be attained.

There were 153 stations, averaging about twelve and a half miles apart. The eating-houses were twenty-five or thirty miles apart, and perhaps as often a small ranch or farm house, whose owner made his living by selling hay to the trains of emigrants and freighters. Every fifty or hundred miles there was a small grocery store and blacksmith shop; and in the '60s, about as frequently a military post, at which a company or two of United States troops for protection against the Indians were stationed.

The buildings and fences along the route were of logs or prairie turfs. The roofs consisted of a foot thickness of sod, sand, clay, and logs or twigs, with an occasional inside lining of skins or thick cloth. The floors were usually the natural soil.

The meals at the stage stations consisted of bacon, eggs, hot biscuits, green tea, coffee, dried peaches and apples, and pies; beef was occasional, and canned fruits and vegetables were furnished at least half the time. The same kind of food was served each meal, and passengers distinguished breakfast, dinner and supper only by the hour.

The first overland mail stage from the Missouri River to Salt Lake City was inaugurated on July 1, 1850, as a monthly service under a four-year Government contract. A mail route was established between Salt Lake City and Sacramento in the early fifties. After some years of irregular service, weekly stages were put on the route in 1858, and in 1861 a daily system was instituted. The first through daily stages on this route left St. Joseph and Placerville simultaneously on July 1 and each made the trip in a few hours over seventeen days. In September the starting point was moved from St. Joseph to

Atchison. Thereafter, a four-horse Concord coach left Atchison every day at eight o'clock in the morning.

The discovery of gold in Colorado in 1858, and the great rush to the new field the following spring, led to the organization of the Leavenworth and Pike's Peak Express by the firm of Jones, Russell, and Company of Leavenworth, for the purpose of putting on a line of stage coaches between that City and Denver. Everything was made ready and the line went into operation in April, 1859. The route ran west from Leavenworth past Indianola, a prominent town in those days situated about two miles northwest of Topeka; it followed the north bank of the Kaw River to Junction City and then went westward along the divide between the Republican and Solomon rivers. The whole length of the road, as first laid out, was 687 miles; this distance was later shortened a few miles. West of Junction City the stations were established at intervals of about twenty-five miles.

Each station was supplied with tents (which were soon to be replaced by houses), of sufficient size to accommodate all the employees and passengers; each tent was occupied by a man and his family. The Company equipped the line with fifty-two Concord coaches, one of which was scheduled to leave each end of the route each day, excepting Sundays, at six A.M., and was to make the trip in ten or twelve days. Every ten days a freight and provisions train was dispatched to distribute supplies to the several stations.[3]

Because of the scarcity of fuel and water west of the Republican and Solomon rivers and because of Indian depredations along the line in July, the route was abandoned a few weeks after it went into operation. The stock and coaches were moved to the Platte River and the stages made trips once a week. The road finally taken was by way of Atchison over the Overland Stage route. The Leavenworth and Pike's Peak

Express was absorbed later by the Overland Stage Line.

The first two westbound coaches on the Leavenworth and Pike's Peak Express arrived in Denver May 7, with nine through passengers aboard, having made the trip from Leavenworth in nineteen days and bringing news from the States down to April 18.

During the rush to the gold field in the spring of 1859, several parties tried to reach Denver by traveling over the Smoky Hill route, that is by way of the Kansas and Smoky Hill rivers. It is said that they were misled by circulars and cards issued in eastern Kansas representing this route as a good road with good camps, and 250 miles shorter than any other route, whereas there was no road west of Salina and very little wood or water. Most of those, who reached their destination, had endured untold hardships; many were found on the plains in an almost famished condition; others died before aid reached them, or left their trains and were not seen again.

Two men from Ohio reported that they had traveled twelve days without seeing wood and one hundred fifty miles without water, excepting for melting snow. For sixty miles, they passed through continuous sand hills where traveling was most difficult. While they were passing over these hills they picked up three men who were dying of hunger and thirst, having eaten nothing for four days. A man arrived at Russellville and reported that his companions, nine in number, had given up and laid down on the prairie some miles distant. A relief party was sent out and found one dead from starvation and two others so far gone that they died soon after reaching the settlement. A few days later a party of thirteen arrived in a starved condition. They had followed the Smoky Hill as far as practicable and then had gone across to the Platte. They were obliged to kill their pack horses and subsist on their flesh. About the same time two footmen reached Denver. They reported having passed ten or fifteen dead

bodies, unburied, and many fresh graves; also many cattle
which had been turned loose on the plains. These men said
that they had lived nine days upon prickly pears and one
hawk.[4] The road was lined with cook-stoves, clothes, and
mining tools that had been thrown out to lighten the loads.
In the absence of grain and grass, many emigrants were forced
to feed flour to their exhausted stock.

In 1865 David Butterfield, a pioneer business man of Denver and later of Atchison, organized a company to open up a
freight and passenger line between Atchison and Denver over
this route. This line was known as the Smoky Hill Route or
Butterfield Overland Despatch. The first coach over this line
left Atchison September 11, 1865, and arrived at Denver on
the morning of the 23rd. Mr. Butterfield accompanied the
coach. The arrival of the stage in Denver was the occasion for
an elaborate reception and banquet in honor of the promoters.
The coach was met four miles up Cherry Creek by a proces-
sion made up of carriages filled with businessmen of Denver
and a cavalcade of horsemen preceded by the First Colorado
Band. A banner in one of the leading carriages bore this inscription: "The energy of our old townsman Col. D. A. Butterfield proves him the Hercules of Expressmen. Welcome
Dave and your Express!"

Colonel Butterfield was taken into the carriage occupied by
the Mayor of Denver and escorted through several of the
principal streets to the Planter House, the band playing lively
and patriotic airs. A crowd gathered in front of the hotel.
Butterfield soon appeared on the veranda and made a short
talk. He stated that the feasibility of the route was shown by
the fact that they came through from "Fort Ellsworth," a
distance of 380 miles in seven days without a change of stock.[5]

Transportation over this route grew rapidly from the start
and the venture would probably have been successful had the
company not suffered great financial loss from Indian attacks.

Consequently, within eighteen months from the inauguration of the enterprise, the entire business and equipment of the Butterfield Company were taken over by Ben Holladay.

Hardships

The drivers and passengers on the stage coaches were subjected to many hardships. The trails, much of the way, led through a desolate country uninhabited except by buffalo and roving bands of Indians. Few white people were seen on the trail except the keepers of the stations, and the occupants of a stage coming from the opposite direction with whom brief greetings were exchanged when the two met. Some of the dangers which faced the traveler on the trail were: Indian attacks, robbers, violent storms, washouts in the road, swollen streams, and broken or overheated axles, or some other part of the vehicle giving out. The roads were frequently in bad shape. The steep grades and precipitous embankments of the mountain roads brought terror to the heart of the timid traveler and thrills and excitement to the fearless one.

Experienced men possessing level heads and good judgment were selected for drivers. The rougher and more dangerous the road the better it seemed to suit them. They built up a reputation of being able to dash over the trail at a lively gait and miss all stones and other obstructions, and to keep the coach right side up while turning sharp curves and going at breakneck speed along steep embankments.

Pleasures

There was also the light and pleasant side of life on the trail. The passengers and drivers passed the long hours telling stories and singing songs. Some of the drivers were fine singers and quite a number of them played musical instruments.

Dances were frequently held at the more important stations. A number of young women attended these dances. Travelers were puzzled to know where so many girls came from out in this "man's country." Often private parties chartered a coach and occupied it by themselves, having a glorious time on the trip.

Tales of the Trails

Out of the hardships and suffering, out of the hairbreadth escapes and thrilling experiences, mingled with pleasure and joy, good times and genial fellowship, came the tales of the trails which are narrated in this chapter.

Indian Attacks

The Indians made serious depredations along the stage routes in the '60s. They were especially aggressive toward the close of the Civil War, burning houses and barns, killing people and running off stock. In 1864 they burned every house along the Overland line for three hundred miles west of the Sandy, murdered eighty settlers, and stole most of the stock. That year the savages destroyed or stole a full half-million dollars worth of property from the Overland Stage Company. The havoc they wrought made food for man and beast along the stage route exceedingly scarce the following winter and spring. The stage company was forced to pay from ten to twelve dollars a bushel for corn which had to be brought from the Missouri and Mississippi valleys, and from seventy-five to one hundred dollars a ton for hay. The price of meals at the stage stations was increased to one dollar and one dollar and a half. A guard of two to four cavalrymen escorted each stage through the exposed parts of the trail as a protection against the Indians. Two regiments of infantry, consisting entirely of former Confederate soldiers, that is prisoners or deserters, were in active service on the plains. They were known in the army as "white-washed rebs," or as they called themselves "galvanized Yankees."

Fight on the Little Blue

On May 18, 1865, a squad of twelve or fifteen soldiers belonging to the Third United States Volunteers on their way from the hospital at Leavenworth to join their regiment on the plains, were marching without arms and were attacked by a body of Indians near Pawnee Station. The Indians came up to them first professing to be friendly. The soldiers received them in a friendly manner until they commenced showing signs of hostility. The sergeant, after the Indians had gathered around the wagon in a threatening manner, ordered the men to seize their arms, jump out and fall in line for defense. The Indians, becoming alarmed at this, quickly retreated, but seeing that the men had no arms, fired and fell upon them, killing two and wounding five or six others. The men defended themselves as best they could until they were overpowered, when all who were able to travel attempted to escape and some managed in this way to save their lives.

The following day a stage coach left the station where the fight had taken place. The driver and passengers were feeling thankful over their fortunate escape from danger when suddenly twenty-five Indians emerged from the bluffs and commenced firing at the coach. They aimed first to kill the horses and prevent the further progess of the vehicle, but in this design they failed. Then they directed their arrows at the coach, at which between 200 and 300 arrows were fired, all without effect. While the horses were running at full speed, three men got on top of the coach and kept up a continuous fire. One Indian was killed, but none of the whites were injured. A running fire was kept up until camp some six or seven miles away was reached, the distance having been covered in about fifteen minutes.[6]

Battle Near Cow Creek

On June 12, 1865, Lieutenant Jenkins of the Second Colorado Cavalry and six men were attacked by about a hundred Indians four miles west of Cow Creek while they were escorting the United States mail coach from Cow Creek to Fort Zarah. Ordering the coach back, Lieutenant Jenkins and his little party stood their ground and fought the savages who charged up within ten feet, slightly wounding two of the soldiers. In the fight one Indian and one pony were killed.

When the coach arrived at Cow Creek, Captain Hammer of the Seventh Iowa Cavalry started immediately with fifty-five men to the scene of action. The Indians had moved in a southwest direction. The whites pursued the savages, and although the latter were two miles in advance, the former overtook them as they were crossing the Arkansas River, killing and wounding at least fifteen of the red skins. Leaving a sergeant and twenty men to guard the crossing, the white troops continued to follow the Indians for three miles south of the river; but being unable to overtake them the soldiers abandoned the pursuit.[7]

Stage Attacked Near Fort Dodge

Peter Kelly was one of the stage coach messengers on the Santa Fe Trail in the '6os. Once, while Kelly and A. L. Carpenter, the stage driver, were making the long ride between Fort Zarah and Fort Dodge, they camped on the plains, kindled a fire of buffalo chips, and ate a hearty meal of broiled buffalo hump, slap jacks and black coffee sweetened with molasses. Then Kelly took Carpenter to one side and said that he did not like the signs he had seen at the Pawnee Fork crossing. He thought that they would have trouble with the Cheyennes before they got to Fort Dodge and added, "So you lay down and get what rest you can and I'll watch out."

Peter knew that the Cheyennes had been following the coach all day, but he did not want to frighten the passengers. He awakened Carpenter at three o'clock next morning and stated that they had better be moving as the Indians probably would attack at daylight. The passengers were aroused, the horses hitched up, and away they went over the prairie.

All the forenoon Peter sat upon the boot, his repeating rifle across his knees his eyes watching the horizon all around. About noon he caught sight of the Indians. They would bob up into sight and down again as they rode in single file over the sand hills about two miles off on the right.

Peter handed the mail sacks from the front boot to the passengers inside the coach and said,

"Barricade the coach sides, boys, with these sacks; they will protect you from arrows and bullets."

Each passenger had one revolver and some had two. They were instructed by Peter to get them ready for action.

Nearer and nearer to the coach came the Indians riding in single file and circling round and round. Peter said to Carpenter,

"You get into the boot and protect yourself. Keep right on the trail, no matter what happens, and don't let the team get away."

As the Indians came nearer, he told the passengers not to waste bullets and to keep their nerve; if they did so victory would be assured.

The arrows and lances came in a shower and several of them hit the coach. Peter changed his seat to the top of the coach. He was a fine target but had a better range and could

shoot more effectively. After the first charge, the Indians retreated, leaving their leader and another member of the band
dead on the ground. The passengers aimed better the second
charge. In this charge another Indian was killed, several were
wounded, and three Indian ponies were disabled. Only five
savages were left, but they charged close to the coach.

Just then the Indians dashed away across the prairie in the
direction whence they came. This surprised the group of
whites. Peter stood up on the coach, and looking around, saw
the cause of this maneuver. Away ahead of the coach coming
toward it was a long train. It was Miguel Otero's ox train of
thirty wagons loaded with wool on the road from Albuquer-
que. The Indians had seen it first, and ran away to hide in the
sandhills.[8]

Raid on the Butterfield Line

On the morning of November 17, 1865, a special coach left
Atchison for a journey across the plains by way of the Butterfield route. The passengers aboard were General Brewster,
vice president of the Butterfield Company; Lawrence Hasbrouck of Kingston, New York; Mr. Calhoun of Atchison;
and Theodore R. Davis, special artist of *Harper's Weekly*.
General Brewster was making the trip for the purpose of putting the stage line in order so as to enable the company to run
their coaches with greater regularity and to make the journey
as convenient as possible for the passengers.

The journey to "Ruthton* Station," southwest of the present site of Hays, Kansas, was almost without incident. The
coach left Ruthton on the evening of the 19th and had barely
reached the next station, Bluffton, when the driver called out

* A study of contemporaneous material shows that this station was on or
near the site of Louisa Springs Station, southwest of Hays, Kansas. A station
called Ruthton was near Denver.

that someone was coming down the road. The passengers
seized their Ballard rifles and prepared them for service. The
newcomers proved to be Mr. Perrin of Denver, the coach
driver who had taken out the last stage; two carpenters; and
a negro blacksmith. They informed the occupants of the
coach that they had been attacked by Indians at Downer Station; three of the party had been killed, one made a prisoner,
and the coach and teams taken.

On receiving this information, they turned back to Ruthton
where a considerable train of wagons, containing provisions
for the Butterfield Company, was parked. The drivers of this
train were armed with Ballard rifles and could withstand any
attack made on them by the Indians.

After they arrived at Ruthton, General Brewster at once
dispatched a messenger to Colonel Tamblyn, commanding
the troops at Big Creek, stating the case and asking for an
escort that they might proceed and discover the extent of the
damage. Colonel Tamblyn came that evening, but too late to
start. Early on the morning of the 21st, they left Ruthton, an
escort of cavalry accompanying the coach and an escort of
infantry going with the train. They found that the station at
Bluffton had been burned and discovered near the station a
number of army wagons without animals of any kind near
them. The Indians had stampeded fifty-seven government
mules and run off with them. They camped that night at
Downer, saw the empty shed; the burnt coach, in which the
Perrin party were riding when the savages attacked them; and
plenty of Indian tracks, but no bodies or fresh graves.

The next day they continued their journey. A short distance from the station, they discovered the remains of Van
Kechten, one of the carpenters with the Perrin party. His body
could properly be called remains, for the wolves had eaten
most of it. They buried what was left. They were told that
one of the stock tenders had been roasted by a slow fire. He

cried so piteously that the red skins cut his tongue out. They camped at Grant Station that night. This station had been evacuated.

The next day the party reached Chalk Bluffs where they found a number of stock tenders, drivers, and others, who had fled from the stations.

On the evening of the 24th, the caravan reached Monument where Captain Stroud had a camp. Leaving this camp on the following morning, the coach, containing General Brewster, and Messrs. Hasbrouck, Perrin, and Davis, started with an escort of five cavalrymen for Smoky Hill Spring Station eleven miles west of Monument. Doctor Whipple, who had come to Monument to dress the wounds of a soldier who had been scalped alive, accompanied the party, with three men in his ambulance.

The coach was within a few moments' drive of the Smoky Hill Spring Station when Davis saw a band of Indians charging on them less than sixty yards distant. The cavalrymen had already arrived at the station and had dismounted.

The moment Davis gave the alarm, he picked up his rifle and sent its contents at the most gaudily dressed Indian who ran off. On the other side of the coach, the General was firing at a white man who appeared to be the leader of the party. He was probably Bill Bent's son. Hasbrouck also tried to shoot the white leader. Perrin was riding outside of the coach when the attack was made. He jumped from the coach and opened fire with his revolver. Between each shot he would remark,

"If I had my old gun full of buck shot!"

The coach had reached the station by this time and the attacking party had retired. Then another band of red skins started for the stock. Seeing this, one of the herders made an effort to drive the stock toward the station. One of the Indians charged on him, shooting arrows at him, and was within a few paces of the herder when Davis fired the contents of his rifle into the Indian's back causing a series of curious gyrations on the part of the savage who was tied to his horse. By this time there was not an Indian within a half-mile of the coach so the white men looked about to discover the next move of the enemy.

They saw the Doctor's ambulance being drawn rapidly over the hills by its four-mule team followed by the Indians who were whipping their worn-out ponies mercilessly. The mules seemed to be gaining ground when several parties of Indians, who seemed to come from every hillside, joined in the chase. The Indians came up on all sides of the ambulance shooting at it, the Doctor and his three men firing an occasional shot with good effect.

The Doctor had been mounted on a splendid horse but had left it and joined the men who had gotten out of the ambulance and were trying to escape on foot.

When Brewster's party saw the men leave the ambulance they determined to help them. The five cavalrymen rode toward them, while two or three of the other men made a diverting attack on another band of savages.

The result was that the Doctor and his companions reached the cavalrymen, mounted behind them, and came into camp.

In a few minutes the Indians, who had captured the ambulance, drove it past the camp at a respectful distance. Sometimes an Indian was on one mule, sometimes on another. The ambulance was completedy loaded down with the scoundrels who were plundering its contents. Doctor Whipple, angered at this, exclaimed,

"I wish I had had a quantity of whisky and strychnine that I could have mixed before I left the ambulance. Anyhow, I dosed the flour with tartar emetic before I left."

The horse that the Doctor rode was a fine one. The Indians had considerable difficulty in capturing the animal. This ac-

complished, they paraded the horse before the whites calling,
"Heap good; mad horse; Whoop! Whoop!" Some of the
men started for them and they ran out of rifle range.

Five of the soldiers, who composed the garrison of the station, were off on a buffalo hunt, thus saving their horses. The
mounts of the other cavalrymen at the station were run off by
the red skins. Just before evening, Brewster's party saw the
five horsemen far in the distance reconnoitering. A few moments later, they saw about thirty Indians dash toward them.
Off went the cavalrymen followed by the savages.

During the night, the white men stood guard. An occasional arrow was sent over their camp for the purpose of discovering their position. That game did not work so the Indians left them.

From the arrows, the party discovered that the savages
were of the Cheyenne and Arapaho tribes. They had been
committing outrages on the Platte and were en route for Fort
Zarah to secure the presents that the government had there
ready for them.

The next morning, Captain Musgrove, of the First U. S.
Volunteers, came to their rescue. He informed them that the
Indians had attacked the troops at Monument but had been
driven off. At about the same time, Captain McMichael arrived from Pond Creek with an escort of his cavalry. General Brewster's party decided to accompany McMichael's
troops to Pond Creek which place they reached the following
evening.[9]

Indian War in 1868

The four Indian tribes of western Kansas, dissatisfied with
the treaty made in 1867 at Medicine Lodge Creek, went on the
war path the following year. Early in August, a party of two

hundred Cheyenne warriors went north from the Pawnee Fork into the valleys of the Saline and Solomon rivers where they committed depredations and then began pillaging and murdering along the trails. On the 23rd, they attacked the stage to Cheyenne Wells on the Smoky Hill route. The stage was forced to return and was followed by thirty Indians for four miles, who kept up a running fire without doing any damage. The situation became so bad that, on the Santa Fe Trail, two coaches were run together three times a week for protection.

A number of wagon trains were attacked. On August 12, the report came from Fort Dodge that one hundred and twenty-nine mules and three horses were run off from a Mexican train at Pawnee Forks on the Santa Fe Trail. Later in the month, another Mexican train suffered a similar experience at the hands of a band of Arapahoes and Cheyennes. Sixteen of the guards were killed and after they were scalped, their bodies were burned with the wagons. Another train, a few miles beyond, successfully resisted the efforts of the savages for its capture. A train loaded with seventy-five thousand pounds of wool was attacked at Cimarron Crossing. The men fought until their supply of ammunition was exhausted and then abandoned the train saving what stock they could. In September a portion of the Seventh Cavalry was sent from Fort Dodge to assist a wood train, consisting of thirty-five wagons and having fifty men with it. They had been fighting for four days. Two men and two horses were killed, seventy-five head of cattle were run off, and a great many mules were wounded. Five and one-half miles farther west, the cavalrymen found the remains of a train of ten wagons that had been captured and burned. Nothing but the iron works remained to tell the story. There had been fifteen persons with the train and it was supposed that they had all been killed and their bodies burned.[10]

Storms

Next to Indian attacks, storms were probably the most serious hardship encountered on the trails. Violent storms frequently came up suddenly and after doing a great deal of destruction passed on as quickly as they came. In summer there were washouts and swollen streams, and the thunder and hail caused the stock to stampede. In winter man and beast were frozen to death by the terrible blizzards that swept the prairie.

Eastern Notables Drenched

In the spring of 1865, the mail companies provided special coaches in which Schuyler Colfax, speaker of the National House of Representatives, crossed the continent. He invited as traveling-companions Messrs. William Bross, Lieutenant-Governor of Illinois; Samuel Bowles, of the Springfield, Massachusetts, *Republican;* and Albert D. Richardson, of the New York *Tribune.* The party was accompanied by George K. Otis of New York, special agent of the Overland Stage Line, as a guide; and by four cavalrymen (all ex-Confederate soldiers), who served as guards.

The party left Atchison on May 22. At Big Sandy, one hundred and forty miles from Atchison, they entered the region of the Indian depredations of the previous year. For three hundred miles every house and barn along the trail had been burned, the stock stolen and scores of people murdered. There were no women and children at the ranches and few soldiers on guard at the stations. At one station they found a mimic cannon which had been used effectually to frighten the Indians. It consisted of a piece of stove pipe mounted on cart wheels.

One morning when they were driving along the banks of the Platte about six miles east of Fort Kearney, a severe storm of thunder and lightning, hail and rain struck them. First, huge rolling clouds massed in the west, presenting a more threatening appearance than any of the party had ever seen. Then a tornado of wind came upon them, overturning emigrant wagons, throwing up vast sheets of water from the Platte and blowing teamsters into and across the stream. Their own horses whirled around with their backs to the storm. Every bit of loose baggage was blown across the prairie. Next hail, as large as bullets, beat down on them. The horses quailed before the terrible pain, then reared and ran, dragging by their bits the men who attempted to hold them. The passengers tumbled out of the coach as rapidly as possible. They saved themselves from one peril but met another—the terrific barrage of hail which bit like wasps and stunned like blows.

A ludicrous incident caused them to forget the storm for a moment. Near them a terrified mule, having thrown his rider, stood with perpendicular ears, expanded nostrils and braced legs, facing the tornado and refusing to move, while in front his master, with braced feet, was pulling with all his strength at the reins.

The drivers and military escort engaged in quite a struggle with the frightened horses, during which the coach came near overturning. After everybody was badly beaten by the hail, it subsided into a pouring rain, the horses were quieted, and the drenched passengers got into the coach and hastened over a prairie flooded with water to the Fort Kearney station.[11]

Lost on the Prairie

Early in March, 1868, a coach, containing six passengers, left Coyote Tuesday morning at 11:40. It was due at Denver on Thursday evening. It had gone only a few miles out of

Coyote when it was overtaken by a blizzard. The wind was
terrible and a blinding snow fell. The driver attempted to return to Coyote but lost the road and was in the midst of the
prairie when night came. He stopped the coach and they remained there all night. The cold was intense but no one was
frozen. The next day they found the road and reached the
first station at half past three o'clock in the afternoon.[12]

Horace Greeley's Overland
Journey to California

When Horace Greeley, the well-known editor of the New
York *Tribune* and candidate for President of the United
States, made his trip from New York to California in 1859, he
spent some time in Kansas and then boarded the stage on the
Pike's Peak Express line for Denver. After visiting the gold
diggings and other points of interest, he followed the trail to
Laramie and the Overland route west through Salt Lake City.

Greeley's trip attracted considerable attention and he had
some noteworthy experiences. He was known to some of the
westerners personally and to most of them by reputation. He
arrived at Atchison May 5; the following day with three companions, he set out in a two-horse wagon, intending to drive
overland to Osawatomie for the purpose of attending the
Republican convention. When they reached Leavenworth,
they were forced, because of the excessive rainfall and high
water in the streams, to take a steam boat down the Missouri
River about fifty miles. On his return trip, he left Osawatomie
by stage May 19 and arrived in Lawrence the following morning. He was met at Wakarusa Creek by a reception committee
headed by Thaddeus Prentice. A cavalcade was formed with
Jonathan Oldham as Marshal who wielded as his baton a copy
of the New York *Tribune*, while many of the horsemen wore
Tribunes in their hats. Greeley stopped at the Eldridge Hotel

and spoke from the steps at three o'clock to an immense crowd which had assembled. Before the banquet, which was served in his honor, was ready, he wandered into the dining room, wearing his muddy boots, and asked for something to eat. The committee had great difficulty getting him out of the room without offending him.

The famous editor returned to Leavenworth on the 23rd and started for the coast the following day, going as far as Manhattan in the Fort Riley stage for the purpose of filling speaking engagements. At Manhattan he joined Albert D. Richardson, who represented the Boston *Journal* and other eastern papers. Richardson had come from Leavenworth on a stage provided by the Leavenworth and Pike's Peak Express Company which furnished free transportation to these noted journalists.

As the two men traveled westward, Greeley was viewed with curious interest by the frontiersmen, was the subject of much comment, and had some thrilling experiences. At one station a farmer asked if Greeley had failed in business and was headed for Pike's Peak to dig gold. Another inquired if he intended to start a newspaper at Manhattan, Kansas. As the stage was leaving another station an Indian girl remarked,

"Horace Greeley in his old white coat is sitting in that coach!"

Out in western Kansas, the coach was stopped by a mired wagon which blocked the road. Several Ohio emigrants were trying to extricate it with their oxen. The noted editor helped them lift the wheels out of the mire. When they paused a moment from their labors, one of the emigrants asked Greeley about the nature of his business. He replied that he was connected with a New York daily journal.

"What journal?"

"The *Tribune*."

"Ah! that's old Greeley's paper, isn't it?"

"Yes sir."

Just then a member of the party, who had been absent, returned, and recognizing the famous New Yorker, said to his comrades,

"Gentlemen, this is Mr. Greeley of New York."

It is needless to say that the curious interrogator was dumb with amazement and chagrin.

Farther west on the trail the mules, while descending a steep hill, became frightened at three Indians and broke a line. They ran down a precipitous bank, upsetting the coach, and galloped away with the fore-wheels. The passengers, with the exception of Greeley, sprang out in time to escape being overturned. From a mass of cushions, carpet-sacks, and blankets, he soon emerged, his head rising above the side of a vehicle. Blood was flowing from cuts in his cheek, arm and leg. He was rescued from his cage and was taken to station Seventeen where his wounds were dressed. This accident caused lameness for some time. After Greeley reached Denver, the limb became so painful that he occupied an empty cabin where he could be free from the noise of the Denver House and obtain the rest needed to recover from the injury. While he was here, Little Raven the noted Arapaho Chief, visited him. When the savage, who measured greatness by a material rule, was being told that Greeley was a literary man and a great editor, he interrupted the explanation to ask how many horses he owned.

The great New Yorker had a perilous ride while crossing the Sierra Nevada Mountains. The road was rocky and sliding, and in many places ran along the edge of dizzy precipices where one looked down for a thousand feet upon patches of green vegetation and threadlike streams below. The giving way of a single stone or a mis-step of six inches in places might have sent the coach rolling over the embankment. The stage was driven by Hank Monk, one of those dare-devil drivers so common on the Overland line, who knew no fear.

Greeley had a lecture engagement in Placerville on the western side of the Sierras, and as the horses climbed slowly up the eastern slope, he feared that he would be late. Twice he urged the driver forward, but the latter paid no attention. Finally they reached the summit and began to descend. Then Monk cracked his whip and the horses at full run tore along the narrow road on the very edge of the precipitous embankment. After having been tossed about in the bounding vehicle for a time, the famous editor assured the driver that such haste was unnecessary, that being half an hour late would make no great difference.

"Keep your seat, Mr. Greeley," replied Monk, with a fresh crack of the whip. "Keep your seat; I'll get you to Placerville in time!"

The journey was accomplished in safety and in time for the lecture. The story of this ride pleased certain Californians so much that they presented Monk with a handsome gold watch, bearing the inscription:

"Keep your seat Mr. Greeley—I'll get you to Placerville in time." [13]

Ben Holladay's "Hold-up"

Holladay's account as given to a New York reporter:

"One night I was bouncing over the plains in one of my overland coaches. Mrs. Holladay and myself were the only passengers. Several stages had been robbed within two months, and the driver was ripping along as though a gang of prairie wolves were after him. Suddenly the horses were thrown on their haunches and the stage stopped. I was heaved forward, but quickly recovered, and found myself gazing at the muzzle of a double-barreled shot gun.

" 'Throw up your hands and don't stir' shouted the owner, in a gruff voice.

"Up went my hands, and I began to commune with myself. The fellow then coolly asked for my money. I saw that he did not know who I was, and I was afraid that my sick wife might awaken and call my name. My coat was buttoned over my bosom, but scarcely high enough to hide a magnificent emerald that cost me over $8,000 a few weeks before in San Francisco. I scarcely breathed through fear that light might strike the stone, and its sparkling brilliancy attract the attention of the robber. I had about $40,000 in a money belt and several hundred dollars in my pockets.

"Suddenly my friend shouted: 'Come shell out quick, or I'll send the old 'un a free lunch.' I passed out the few hundreds loose in my pockets and handed him my gold watch and chain. They were heavy. I think the chain alone would weigh five pounds at least.

" 'There,' said I, 'there's every cent I've got! Take it and let me go. My wife is very ill, and I don't know what would happen if she knew what was going on.'

" 'Keep your hands up!' was the reply, while a second robber received my watch and money.

"Then a search was made for the express company's box, but the double-barreled shotgun did not move. Its muzzles were within a foot of my nose. For my life I did not dare to stir. My nose began to itch. The stiff hairs of my moustache got up, one after another, and tickled it, until the sensation was intolerable. I could stand it no longer.

" 'Stranger,' I said, 'I must scratch my nose! It itches so that I am almost crazy.'

" 'Move your hands,' he shouted, 'and I'll blow a hole through your head big enough for a jack-rabbit to jump through!'

"I appealed once more! 'Well,' he answered, 'keep your hands still and I'll scratch it for you.'

" 'Did he scratch it?' asked one of Ben's interested listeners.

" 'Sure,' said Mr. Holladay.

" 'How?' asked the breathless listener.

" 'With the muzzle of the cocked gun,' said the great over-lander. 'He rubbed the muzzle around my moustache and racked it over the end of my nose until I thanked him and said that it itched no longer.'

"The robbers soon afterwards took their leave, with many apologies and I continued my journey to the Missouri river with the big emerald and $40,000." [14]

Record Stage Trips

As stated above, the stage made the regular trip between Independence and Santa Fe, a distance of nearly eight hundred miles, in about fourteen days; they covered the nineteen hundred miles from Atchison to Placerville in a few hours over seventeen days, and went from Atchison to Denver on the Smoky Hill route in about twelve days. When Horace Greeley made his trip to the coast over the Leavenworth and Pike's Peak line, the coach made from twenty-eight to sixty-eight miles per day.

Several record trips were made by stage. One of the fastest on record was made by Ben Holladay in the summer of 1864. He visited his overland line twice a year and when he did, he usually disregarded expense and rules relative to speed. Holladay made the record-breaking ride shortly after the disaster to the steamer Golden Gate on the Pacific shore in which his partner, Edward R. Flint, lost his life and he himself narrowly escaped a watery grave. He rode by special coach from San Francisco to Atchison in twelve days and two hours, having driven from Salt Lake to Atchison, twelve hundred and twenty miles, in six and one-half days.

This was an expensive ride for the stage king, costing him

about $20,000 in wear and tear of coaches and injury to and loss of horses. However, it proved to be a great advertisement for his stage line. Being the quickest trip ever made across the plains in a Concord coach, the press over the country wrote it up to the advantage of the Overland line. The only ride over the plains comparable to this was the one made by François Xavier Aubry on horseback from Santa Fe to Independence, an account of which is found in another place.

Schuyler Colfax and his party crossed the continent in the spring of 1865 by way of the Platte valley route, reaching Denver in four and a half days from the time they left Atchison. This journey constituted a great triumph in stage management. When they reached one station the driver said to the waiting hostlers,

"Gents, we are four hours behind and want to make up the time. We must change these teams in three minutes by the watch." [15]

The Man on Horseback
F. X. Aubry's Record Horseback Rides

Several noted rides were made in the Old West. The stories of these rides are a part of the romance of the frontier. The pony express riders will always be heroes of the saddle. Much has been said and written about their conquests in the field of speed and endurance, and about the perfection of their organization. For instance Buffalo Bill Cody exhibited his power of endurance and kept the mail going forward when he rode from Red Buttes to Three Crossings, and finding the rider there dead, continued on to Rocky Ridge, eighty-five miles away, reaching each relay station on time, and then rode back to Red Buttes; he covered three hundred and twenty-two miles which is the longest pony express journey on record. A few years later Cody carried dispatches for General Sheridan between four Kansas forts and rode three hundred fifty-five miles in fifty-eight hours.

The greatest ride in history was made by François Xavier Aubry,* a Santa Fe trader, when Cody and other pony express riders were children. He made three famous rides over the Santa Fe Trail in 1847 and 1848, largely in the interests of his business. The third is the greatest ride recorded in history. The accounts of his rides are buried in files of old newspapers and as a result they have largely escaped the notice of the present generation of readers, though contemporary writers called his rides "Unprecedented—Space almost annihilated."

Aubry was by birth a French Canadian. He was a wiry little man, five feet two inches tall and weighed one hundred pounds. In the early period, he came to St. Louis and got a job in a carpet store. Here he heard glowing tales of the Southwest told by those engaged in the Santa Fe trade. Lured by these stories, he went to Independence and joined one of the outfits. In a short time he became an independent trader, made several trips over the trail, and was well known in Missouri and throughout the West.

He was a venturesome individual who did things a little earlier and a little faster than his competitors. Not many years before he made his rides, a journey on horseback to Santa Fe required from twenty to thirty days and it was believed impossible for traders to make two trips the same season, yet it was done. Aubry decided that he could reduce the time required to cross the plains and possibly make three trips to Santa Fe the same season.

On December 22, 1847, he started from Santa Fe, accompanied by five horsemen and his servant. A short distance from that city his party was attacked by a band of Mexican robbers who stole ten of his mules. Nothing daunted thereby

* Spelled also Aubrey.

he raced his horse down the trail. The five men were unable to keep pace with him, though he was detained two days on the road. He passed Fort Mann in the night. When he was within sixty miles of Council Grove his servant gave out; he went on alone and arrived at Independence on January 5, having made the eight-hundred mile trip in fourteen days. The journey was actually performed in twelve days. The press heralded this as the quickest trip across the plains on record.

He got together a fine and well selected stock of goods and departed for Santa Fe on March 16. This was the first time that a wagon train had set out so early in the year. Many predicted the failure of this adventure, but Aubry believed that "fortune favors the brave" and went on with his plans. While he incurred heavy expense by starting so early, he possessed the advantage of reaching the market ahead of the other traders.

The outfit reached Santa Fe in due time and the owner sold his entire stock. Then he returned to Independence on horseback. He left Santa Fe on May 19th and arrived at Independence before sunrise on the 28th, making the journey in eight days and ten hours. He killed three horses and two mules on the trip, walked forty miles, was three days without provisions, and slept only four hours and a half on the route. He averaged 150 miles per day.

This ride, in which the ambitious trader bettered his first record by almost six days, attracted considerable attention all the way from Missouri to New Mexico.

His business compelled him to make another trip and to arrive in the States in the shortest possible time. He believed that he could beat his second record and is said to have bet a sum of money (some say $1,000; others $5,000), that he could make the ride to Independence in six days. The money was covered.

Aubry made preparations at once. It was to be a lone ride. He sent men ahead with relay horses. He completed his preparations and was ready to set out on his record-breaking ride on the morning of September 12. Just before he started, he visited the office of the Santa Fe *Republican*. Editor J. A. Donhoe hastily ran off an Extra which Aubry carried all the way to Missouri. In regard to the rider and his proposed journey, the Editor made the following statement in the Extra:

"Mr. F. X. Aubry, who has this moment left our office and who has just informed us that he is to leave for the United States in a few moments; therefore we strike off a few items of the latest dates and news about town, etc., for the benefit of our exchanges in the states, as we are informed by him that his business compels him to reach the States as soon as he possibly can. We wish him a safe trip and a safe return as we would be happy to see our country settled by just such men as Mr. Aubry—energy and perseverance is what we know is wanted in a new country like this. We would not be surprised to hear that Mr. A. has made the quickest trip this time that ever was made, as his anxiety for his business will induce him to travel at the utmost speed."

Aubry put the newspaper in a safe place, sprang to the saddle, and galloped out of Santa Fe down the mountain road through Pecos and on to Las Vegas, a distance of seventy-four miles, where there were fresh horses. He changed again at Point of Rocks. When he reached the place where the next relay horses were to be, he found that the Indians had killed his man and taken the horses. He was forced to ride on to the Cimarron, 150 miles from Point of Rocks, where there were three fresh horses. He mounted one and drove the other two ahead. As he neared the Arkansas River, the last of the three horses gave out. The noted rider hid the saddle and blanket in the grass, and walked and trotted down the trail for twenty miles until he reached the crossing of the Arkansas which is still called "Aubry's Crossing." Here a fresh horse awaited him.

At Fort Mann Aubry had to see a man on important business. The man was away hunting buffalo. He laid down and slept a couple of hours while he waited.

He rode into Independence in the evening of September 17, having made the ride in the unprecedented short space of time of five days and sixteen hours. The rider had to be lifted from the saddle. His words were in a whisper and the saddle was caked with blood. He had killed six horses on the journey, walked twenty miles, and slept two hours and a half; but he had won his bet and had established a record which has never been surpassed.

After a brief rest, he went on to St. Louis, arriving in that city in the evening of September 22, and delivered the Extra Santa Fe *Republican* to the Editor of the St. Louis *Daily Union*. He made the entire trip from Santa Fe to St. Louis in ten days which was also an unprecedented feat.

Aubry's life came to a tragic end in 1854. He had engaged in freighting on the plains for four or five years and during this time became a close friend of Major R. H. Weightman, editor of the Santa Fe *Herald*. Then he took a flock of sheep to California which proved a great financial success. He explored the country between Santa Fe and southern California and discovered a much better route than those then in use. Another man, who saw the necessity of a new route, followed Aubry. Returning to Santa Fe ahead of him, the man claimed credit for the discovery of the route and induced Weightman to publish an account of the discovery in his paper. Aubry heard of this and was furious. He returned to Santa Fe on August 18 and dismounting, entered the Fonda Hotel where a group of admirers surrounded him. Major Weightman entered the hotel, and as was the custom in the Old West, the crowd moved toward the bar as the congratulations were exchanged. Aubry and Weightman each ordered brandy. The former raised his glass to his lips and then putting it down said to the latter,

"What has become of your paper?"

The Major answered, "Dead."

"What killed it?" asked Aubry.

"Lack of support," was the reply.

"The lie it told on me killed it," Aubry retorted.

Weightman threw the contents of his glass in Aubry's face. The champion horseman, blinded by the liquor, made an effort to draw his gun. The Major quickly drew his knife and stabbed his opponent. The latter dropped to the floor and died almost instantly.

Aubry has been honored by having his name perpetuated in a steamboat on the Missouri River and in several place-names. Five years after the famous ride, the newest and fastest steamboat on the Missouri River was named the *F. X. Aubrey*. On her hurricane roof, aft of the pilot-house, there was carved the figure of a man on horseback. This boat plied the Missouri for some years and provided transportation for many Free State settlers who were on their way to Kansas. Aubry's Crossing has been mentioned. He explored and marked a route from the Arkansas River to Santa Fe which was known as the "Aubrey Route." It left the Arkansas a few miles west of the "Gold Banks" and followed a course midway between the Raton and Cimarron routes. The longest distance between water on this route was thirty miles; on other routes sixty miles. The town of Aubrey on the line between Hamilton and Kearney counties was named in his honor. Aubry discovered the spring of water four miles east of where Syracuse now stands. Fort Aubrey was established at this spring not far from the present village of Mayline late in August or early in September, 1865, but was abandoned the following year.[16]

The Pony Express

Several famous rides were made by the Pony Express which was the first fast mail line between St. Joseph, Missouri, and San Francisco, California. This mail route was organized early in 1860 by William H. Russell and his associates and was in existence eighteen months. Russell purchased a large number of the fleetest horses that he could find and distributed them along the route at intervals of nine to fifteen miles, depending on the nature of the country. He procured the services of one hundred twenty-five men, eighty of whom were for post riders and were selected because they were hardy and light of weight. Each rider was supposed to ride three horses in succession, changing animals at each station, and was expected to go at least thirty-three and one-third miles. Two minutes were allowed for changing horses.

When the promoters had everything in readiness, Russell announced through the press that the first courier of the Pony Express would leave the Missouri River at 5 o'clock in the afternoon of April 3rd and that dispatches would be delivered in San Francisco in eight days and letters in ten days.

The first trip was the most spectacular of the rides made over the route. The announcement that the line was to be opened on April 3rd caused a great crowd to assemble on the streets of St. Joseph to witness the event. Flags were flying and a brass band was playing. A special train over the Hannibal and St. Joseph railroad brought the throughmail from the East into the city. The pouches were rushed to the postoffice where the mail for the Pony Express was made ready.

The pony and its rider were to start from the old Pike's Peak livery stable south of Patee Park. The crowd gathered about this building to watch the courier, Johnnie Frey, a wiry little man scarcely twenty years old, prepare to mount his pony and set out in this race against time across the continent. Everything was ready. All were hushed with subdued expectancy. The time set for the departure had arrived. A cannon boomed in the distance—the starting signal. The rider leaped to his saddle and started up the street. In less than a minute, he reached the postoffice where the pouch containing the letters and documents was put in his charge; without a moment's delay, he arrived at the Missouri River wharf where the ferryboat was waiting. He rode on to the boat and was ferried across the stream. Scarcely had the gang plank been lowered when horse and rider dashed over it and were off on the trail at a furious gallop. Frey rode to Seneca, a distance of sixty miles, in about six hours. Here he was relieved by the rider for the next "stage."

The route from St. Joseph, followed on this initial trip, was to Kennekuk, then northwest across the Kickapoo Indian reservation, through Log Chain, Seneca, Guittard's, Marysville and Hollenberg, and up the Little Blue River valley; the courier crossed the Nebraska line near Rock Creek, went on through Big Sandy, Liberty Farm, and over the prairie to Thirty-two mile Creek; thence to the Platte River, up this river to Fort Bridger, Salt Lake City, Carson City, and finally arrived at Sacramento, nine days and twenty-three hours from the time Johnnie Frey left St. Joseph.

As the courier neared Sacramento, he was met on the road by all who could secure a horse or mule to ride and escorted into town by this cavalcade where he was received with a great ovation—bells were rung, cannons and guns fired, and the populace shouted and waved their hats and handkerchiefs as the rider came down the street. At Sacramento the mail was taken by a steamer down the Sacramento River to San Francisco. The Pony Express had reduced the time for letters from

New York to the coast from twenty-three to less than ten days.

On April 3rd, at about the same hour that Johnnie Frey started from St. Joseph, a pouch of east-bound mail was placed on board a steamer at San Francisco and taken up the river to Sacramento where the first rider for the East was to start. At Sacramento the event was celebrated in a more elaborate manner than at St. Joseph. Magnificent floral decorations lined the streets, bands played, guns were fired and speeches were made. That night, Harry Roff, the first rider for the East, left the city. The first twenty miles were covered in fifty-nine minutes; he changed horses once with a delay of only ten seconds. He changed again at Folsom and then rode on fifty-five miles farther to Placerville, where "Boston," the next courier, took the mail pouch and was off for Friday Station on the other side of the Sierra Nevada range. Seven more changes of riders were made before the mail was carried into Salt Lake City on April 7 at 11:45 P.M.

All went well along the route until the crossing of the Platte River at Julesberg was reached by the courier who found the river bank full and a strong current running. Horse and rider plunged into the stream but only the man reached the opposite bank. His steed mired in the quicksand and perished. The courier saved his mail pouch, and commandeering a mount rode to the next relay station.

When the rider from the West reached Seneca, Johnnie Frey was waiting for him to arrive. He was an hour late and Frey had to make up this time. As the hour drew near for Frey's arrival in St. Joseph, thousands of people lined the river bank gazing with expectancy in the direction of the Kansas woods from which the horse and rider would emerge into the open country one mile from the finish. A youngster was the first to catch sight of the courier and the yell that went up from the crowd reached the ears of the rider a mile away. Horse and rider fairly flew over the ground. Feathery flecks of foam streaked the flanks of the panting animal as she bore the courier to his journey's end, covering the last mile in one minute and fifty seconds. The San Francisco mail was delivered at the Overland office at 3:55 o'clock the afternoon of April 13.[17]

The second east-bound pony express reached St. Joseph at 5 o'clock, April 20—just ten days on the road.[18]

Freight and Emigrant Trains

Prior to 1824 goods were transported over the Santa Fe Trail on the backs of horses and mules. In 1824 a party left Independence with a large number of pack animals and twenty-five wagons loaded with goods. From this time wagon-trains became the usual mode of transportation over all the western trails. In the fifties and early sixties, the overland freighting business was enormous. A considerable portion of the freighting was done by the well-known firm of Russell, Majors and Waddell. Their establishment was located outside of Leavenworth between the fort and the city. Horace Greeley, who saw the headquarters of this firm in May, 1859, left this description:

". . . Such acres of wagons! such pyramids of extra axle-trees! such herds of oxen! such regiments of drivers and other employees! No one who does not see can realize how vast a business this is, nor how immense are its outlays as well as its income. I presume this great firm has at this hour two millions of dollars invested in stock, mainly oxen, mules and wagons. (They last year employed six thousand teamsters, and worked forty-five thousand oxen.)[19] . . . ."

When the overland transportation business was at its height, this firm owned more than 6,200 huge wagons each built to carry from 5,000 to 7,000 pounds of merchandise, and worked 75,000 head of oxen. If the oxen were yoked together and hitched to the wagons, this would make a train approximately forty miles long.

The drivers of the wagon train and the animals, which drew the wagons, endured many hardships. The roads were bad in many places and the wagons frequently stuck in the mud, or the drivers were caught in blizzards and frozen to death in winter. There was the ever-present danger of an Indian attack. Dry murrain, a disease fatal to cattle, sometimes spread among the stock and resulted in heavy loss. In the fall of 1854, this disease made its appearance in the herds owned by Russell, Majors and Waddell, and they lost sixty or seventy head of the best cattle on the road out of their outbound trains.[20] Men and animals often suffered from hunger and thirst. Dead bodies of men and fresh graves were seen along the roadside and many cattle were turned loose on the plains. During the winter of 1865-66, it was estimated that not less than ten thousand head of oxen were frozen to death on the three great routes, the Overland, Butterfield, and the Santa Fe. Instances were numerous of trains meeting with the loss of two-thirds of their stock during a single night. Seventy-five white men were murdered and scalped on the Smoky Hill route in 1867. Twenty-seven Cheyenne Indians were known to have bit the dust that year. The number of Sioux and Arapahoes killed was not known.

Council Grove

Council Grove, located on the Santa Fe Trail about 150 miles from Independence, was a favorite rendezvous of wagon and emigrant trains bound for Santa Fe. The Grove was about fifteen miles from north to south and from one to three miles in width, and consisted chiefly of walnut, hickory, oak and sycamore. In regard to the wood creatures and plant life inhabiting this timbered spot, a contemporary writer of prairie lore writes as follows:

"Among the branching groins and under the leafy roof of this noble prairie cathedral, the mock-bird, brown thrush, the king bird, the beautiful oriole, blue-bird, dove and robin, with many another tenant of the shade, breed in safety, and make the sweet summer air vocal with their matinal song; while over the parterre of yellow and white primrose and beautiful lynchis at the roots of the trees, the humming-bird, splendid dragon-fly, and that fairy-bee the lady-bird, wander by in quest of honey-loves; and on decaying trunks the lusty squirrel sits erect and chatters to the hunter in familiar and happy ignorance that he is good to eat, or needed on the table where all creation seems to speak, Enough." [21]

In the early days of the Santa Fe trade, parties usually assembled at this grove and organized into caravans by electing officers and adopting a code. At a later date, most of the wagon trains delayed here a day or more to rest the animals while the men procured timber for axle-trees and other repairs for the wagons, as there was no serviceable timber near the trail beyond this grove. Logs were tied under the wagons and at times carried all the way to Santa Fe and back again.

The historians say that Council Grove is so called from the fact that the United States Commission and the chiefs of the Indian tribes interested ratified a treaty at this place in 1825 guaranteeing the right of way for the Santa Fe Trail. The Indians have a legendary history of this grove which is more beautiful than the white man's prosaic explanation. They say that many years ago all the prairie and mountain tribes, who were at peace with one another, were wont to meet here each year at the close of the hunting season to celebrate their festival dances and to smoke the peace pipe. While the festivi-

ties were held, the flames from the council fires curled
upwards through the trees—whence the name Council Grove.

Government Train Attacked at Pond Creek

Monument Station, which was abandoned late in February,
1866, for want of subsistence stores, was re-occupied a few
days later by two companies of the First United States Volun-
teer Infantry. Pond Creek, fifty miles west, was garrisoned at
the same time by a company of the Second United States
Cavalry—the old Second Dragoons who did such valiant service in Mexico.

A government train hauling lumber from Denver for the
construction of quarters for the troops at Pond Creek,
reached that place on Monday, March 5. During the night
the cattle were stampeded while they were grazing near the
camp. In the morning the herdsmen were sent out to find the
missing stock. Two of them followed the road to the east and
on going into a deep ravine, came suddenly upon a large body
of Indians who were moving south toward the Arkansas with
their lodges and squaws.

As there was no chance to escape, the herdsmen determined
to sell their lives as dearly as possible. Dismounting from their
horses, they awaited the attack of the Indians who commenced circling about them on their ponies, letting their arrows fly from time to time as they drew nearer.

Suddenly a man, who appeared to be the leader of the savages, gave orders to the Indians to cease firing. Laying down
his own arms, he made signs to the white men that they should
not be molested and started toward them. When he came
nearer, one of the herdsmen recognized him as a Wyandote
half-breed named Guerrier whom he had seen at Fort Lyon
the previous fall. This recognition undoubtedly saved their
lives.[22]

Mormon Grove

In the fifties, companies of Saints were recruited at points near Atchison, Leavenworth and Kansas City and traveled west over the trail used by the Overland Stage. Mormon Grove, situated on the prairie four and a half miles west of Atchison, was a recruiting station; it was a temporary settlement founded in 1855 as an outfitting place for emigrating Saints. That year hundreds of teams and over 3,000 Mormons left this place on their westward journey.

The site of Mormon Grove was selected in March, 1855. Early in April, a number of wagons arrived on the site, and during the spring and summer, companies of Saints arrived at or departed from this place every few days. The last company left for the Great Salt Lake valley August 31 that year. After that date, Mormon Grove was almost deserted; the Saints emigrating from Europe in 1856 landed at New York and traveled west to Iowa City by rail, from which point they departed in wagons for the promised land. Mormon Grove has disappeared. Here and there one can see traces of the old ditches which enclosed the pasture lands and kept the stock from straying away. The little cemetery bears mute testimony that not all the emigrants reached the great valley where they hoped to find peace and happiness.[23]

Counting Stops an Indian Attack

When Rufus B. Sage was crossing the prairies, he and his friend Grin, on one occasion, went some miles out of sight of their caravan in search of stampeded animals with which to recruit his teams. Upon descending a ridge into the hollow beyond, they were confronted by a party of Pawnees. The white men immediately turned their horses around and galloped back the way they had come. The Indians started pursuit and soon their arrows were whistling in the air near them. Then the two men began to speculate on the number of the savages.[24]

"There are five hundred of the devils!" exclaimed Grin to his companion.

"There are not forty," said Sage.

"Twenty dollars on it that there are forty," was the rejoinder.

"Twenty dollars then is the figure," said Sage. Without slackening their speed for an instant, the men shook hands in confirmation of the bet.

"And now, how are we to know who wins?" was the query.

"I'll count them!" said Grin; and wheeling full upon the face of the assailants, and extending the forefinger of his left hand, while his right grasped a revolver, he deliberately began counting, "One, two, three, four," and so on.

Surprised at this turn of affairs, the foremost Pawnee, almost within scalping distance, drew in his pony; the others came to a halt; then seized with dismay at the assurance which enabled a lone man upon the prairie to face their charge, their hearts failed them, and they bolted off at every point.

"Eighteen, nineteen, twenty, twenty-one, twenty-two"; and the lank finger of the trader slowly wagged in the direction of the receding forms, as Sage, taking a curve, came around to his aid. "Thirty-seven, thirty-eight, thirty-nine!" he uttered, with animation, as the last Indian dodged behind the crest of the mound; and turning with a complacent smile—"There must have been forty; who wins?"

"Make it a draw game, and I'll stand treat," answered Sage; and the chums continued their quest for water and grass.

A Shrewd Business Transaction

Alexander Majors, a member of the well-known firm of Russell, Majors and Waddell, overland freighters, was recognized as a shrewd business man among white business men. Probably the nerviest deal he ever consummated was transacted with the Indians on the plains when he held out until they made a ninety per cent reduction in their demands, though an arrow was aimed at his heart all the while, and he was being threatened with death.

In June, 1850, Majors started from Independence to Santa Fe with a train of ten wagons drawn by one hundred thirty oxen. They arrived at 110 Creek and camped for the night. The following morning Majors went out to get the oxen and found that some were gone. He was not armed, but started out to find the missing cattle. He followed the trail until he saw the oxen guarded by six Indians who had dismounted. Majors was hidden from view by the trees so he was not seen until he was near the savages. He gave several loud yells and started the oxen back toward camp. The Indians were so surprised that they did not follow. When he had gotten about half way back to camp, he saw twenty-five warriors approaching. Some of them chased him away, but he returned. This was repeated three times. Then he was approached by the chief and a warrior. The latter tried to seize his horse's reins but failed. Then they approached Majors, the warrior with arrow drawn and pointing toward his heart. The chief by sign language told Majors that his life would be spared if he would give him ten oxen. He refused to do so. Next the savage held up five fingers. Again the freighter refused. Then the demand for three was rejected. The chief now asked Majors to name the number. The latter held up one finger. The Indians drove off one at a furious pace, leaving Majors and the rest of the oxen standing on the prairie. They feared that the white man's friends would come. Majors reached camp about noon.[25]

A German Farmer's Loss

In the fall of 1864, an ox train of seventy-five or eighty loaded wagons bound for the mountains became stuck in the mud a few miles east of the Kickapoo Indian reservation. The train was from Leavenworth, and having been caught in a protracted rain, had become stalled, on the old military road between Atchison and Kennekuk. The wheels had sunk to the hubs in the mud, and even with the four or five yoke of cattle to each vehicle it was impossible for the beasts to pull them out. All that could be done under the circumstances was to unyoke the cattle and turn them loose. This occurred near a cornfield belonging to a German farmer. The cattle had had a hard day's haul and were hungry. As soon as they were un-yoked and let loose, they made a mad rush, broke down the farmer's fence and began devouring the corn. All attempts to drive the hungry animals out proved useless. They not only stayed there all night, but for the next forty-eight hours or more, used the field for a corral. In all there were between 500 and 600 head of oxen, but neither the farmer nor the drivers could do anything with them.

The farmer protested, in broken English, more forcible than elegant, but that did not get the cattle out of the corn field. He finally withdrew, consulted some of his neighbor-hood friends, and after making a careful examination, they estimated that the corn had been damaged to the amount of $250.

He then called on the wagon-boss and said, "You owes me $250. Your oxen eats up mine corn-field and me damaged dot much; I vants mine pay!"

"All right," said the wagon-boss, "I am going to Leavenworth on the first stage and will report the facts to headquarters."

The train-boss left, and returned the following day, bringing the pleasing information that the owner of the train would be up the next day and settle. He came, and the German was on hand to meet him.

"Good morning," said the owner of the train, "I notice that my cattle have not been lacking for something good to eat the past three days."

"Dot ish so," said the German, "and you owes me $250," he said, as he handed his bill to the freighter.

"All right," said the owner of the cattle as he pulled out one $50 and two crisp $100 greenbacks, telling the farmer to receipt the bill, which was promptly done. The freighter politely thanked the German because his cornfield was so close by and that the account was so reasonable, adding, "If you had made the bill $500 I would have paid it just as quickly, and thought, under the circumstances, I was getting out of a dilemma extremely easy. Good day, sir."

"Good day," said the farmer, "but I vants to say, mister, dot I'm von tam Dutch fool. I now see I've lost $250 by mine ignorance. I vish some von vould kick me."

The freighter went to his train, and the German started to the house with his $250; but nearly every step of the way he made the air blue with his German-English maledictions, as he hurried to report to his wife. She was equally interested with her husband in knowing that his bill of $250 was so promptly paid. She saw him coming and met him at the gate. He had the money in his hand, and shaking it before her eyes, said, "Katrina, did you know dot I ish von tam Dutch fool? I vants you to kick me off dis blace. I lose $250; dot man tell me he pay $500 shoost so quick as he pay $250. Eef I been a Yankee I'd been a rich man instead of being a poor tam Dutch

fool. Kick me, Katrina, for not being a Yankee. I feel shoost
like I take a gun and shoots the top of mine head off. Such tam
foolishness make me sick; $250 lost shoost because I was von
honest man. All I know now ish dot I vas von tam Dutch
fool." [26]

Snakes

The great abundance of snakes was an extremely unpleasant
feature of life on the prairie frontier. Pioneer literature is full
of snake stories. While camping out, one frequently felt one
of these reptiles crawl over him in the night or saw one un-
pleasantly near him in the morning. In homes where there
were openings in the floor, the inmates were occasionally
startled to see a rattler peer up through a crack and stare about
the room. It was not an uncommon thing for a farmer, while
stacking wheat, to find fifteen or twenty rattlesnakes under
the shocks when he loaded a hay rack with bundles. Snake
hunts were staged, on which occasions the men and boys of a
community turned out prepared to kill the reptiles. [27]

Bull snakes were able to crawl up the wall of a sod-house
and in hot weather enjoyed the protection from the sun af-
forded by the cool wall. While changing positions the snake
sometimes lost his balance and fell. It is needless to say that
everyone was startled and the settler and his family were
greatly mortified when they and their guests were seated at
the table enjoying a Sunday dinner and a bull snake toppled
off the wall and landed in the gravy.

Rattlesnakes were abundant along the trails, often biting
the mules and oxen when they were grazing. Mules would die
or become useless after being bitten. Freight and emigrant
trains came upon perfect dens of these reptiles where hundreds, if not thousands, were coiled and crawling in every direction. There was seldom to be found either stick or stone
with which to kill them. Therefore, as soon as they were dis-

covered, every man seized a rifle, pistol or whip and was upon them. There was a popping of guns on every hand lest some of the reptiles should get away or bite the stock.

Mirages

Mirages were frequent on the trails. They assumed all manner of fantastic shapes. Objects seen from the distance were way out of proportion. On one occasion, some travelers met a group of mounted men. When they first came in sight the horses' legs looked to be several feet long and the bodies of the horses and their riders extended into the air about fifty feet. In another instance, a herd of buffalo took on the appearance of large camels in a desert.

The Caches

Messrs. McKnight, Beard and Chambers, with a dozen comrades, started with a supply of goods across the plains and by good luck they arrived safely at Santa Fe. The Mexicans arrested the entire party as spies and put them in prison. Beard and Chambers, having by some means escaped, returned to St. Louis in 1822 and told of the prospects of trade with the Mexicans in such glowing terms that they induced some individuals to fit out another expedition with which they again set out for Santa Fe.

It was late in the season; they reached the crossing of the Arkansas without difficulty, but at that point a violent snow storm overtook them and they were compelled to stop and were obliged to remain for more than three months, during which time most of their animals died for want of food and from the severe cold. When the weather had moderated sufficiently to allow them to proceed on their journey, they had no transportation facilities for their goods and were com-

pelled to hide them in pits dug in the earth on the north side of
the Arkansas a few miles east of the site of Fort Dodge. This
method of secreting valuables is called *caching* from the
French word "to hide."

After caching their goods, the party went on to Taos
where they bought mules, and returning to the caches, transported the goods to market.

The place where Beard's expedition wintered was called
"The Caches" for a long time. For many years these mossy
pits could be seen and most travelers on the trail visited them.[28]

Treasure Legend of the Santa Fe Trail

The stories of buried treasures along the trails have resulted, in some instances, in a long and expensive search for
the lost riches. The legend of silver buried by a Spanish
trader named Jesus M. Martinez a few miles west of Dodge
City led to an extended search for the precious metal.

In the summer of 1853, a freighting train, consisting of
eighty-two men with one hundred twenty wagons in charge
of Martinez, was going eastward along the Santa Fe Trail to-
wards Independence, Missouri, where they intended to purchase goods. One evening they halted at sundown about four
miles west of the present site of Dodge City and formed the
usual corral with their wagons. Some time during the night
the men on guard duty observed objects not far from camp.
The dogs began making a fuss, so they awoke Martinez who
decided that Indians were lurking around. He awoke some of
his men. They decided to prepare for the worst and commenced digging trenches and preparing for defense. The
objects around them seemed to grow more numerous and before long could be seen on all sides. Having intrenched themselves, the Mexicans waited. Finally with yells the Indians
made an attack. The eighty-two guns poured fatal balls into

the enemy at every report. The Indians fell back, but renewed the attack at intervals. For five days the siege continued. During this time the Mexicans had scarcely slept and their ammunition was nearly gone. On the sixth night, the Indians made a more desperate attack. As long as their ammunition lasted, the Mexicans continued their resistance, but the supply of powder and lead decreased until none was left. Only one man, Jesus M. Martinez, is known to have escaped. The Indians pillaged the train of all food stuffs, took the stock, set fire to the wagons, and then left. Martinez remained in his hiding place until morning when he made a search for the silver stored in one of the wagons and found a portion of it. As near as he could remember, when he related the occurrence to his son, he found twenty-one bags each containing 1,000 Mexican silver dollars, which he buried. Then he started out and made his way on foot to Mexico where he soon died. Before his death he told his son about the buried treasure.

Young Martinez came to this country some years after his father's death for the purpose of finding the silver. He revealed the secret to two men, one of whom helped in his search. For weeks they searched but were unsuccessful. Finally Martinez returned to Mexico. After he left one of his assistants hired men and set them to digging for the treasure. They found nothing and abandoned the work.[29]

Bullwhackers

The drivers of the ox teams were called "bullwhackers." They were regarded by many as the "toughest individuals on earth" and were proud of this distinction. They were experts at lariat and whip-throwing. The whip consisted of a hickory stalk two feet long, a lash twelve feet in length with buck or antelope-skin snapper nine inches in length. The bullwhacker held the stalk in his left hand and coiled the lash with his right hand and the index finger of the left. Then he whirled the whip several times around his head, letting it shoot straight out and bringing it back with a jerk. It would strike wherever aimed, cutting through the hide and into the flesh of an animal, or would abstract a small piece from the trousers of a tenderfoot without disturbing his flesh. When thrown into space the whip made a report like a gun being fired.[30]

"Our Firm Doesn't Make That Point"

The firm of Russell, Majors and Waddell, overland freighters, required a pledge of every employee that he would not drink intoxicating liquors or use profane language. Alexander Majors of this firm rigidly enforced these requirements when he employed men. One day a bullwhacker entered his office and asked for a job.

"Can you drive oxen?" asked Majors.

"Yep," replied the bullwhacker, "I can drive oxen to hell and back."

"Well, well," replied the veteran freighter, "I can't use you, because our firm doesn't make that point." [31]

A Surprised Tenderfoot

Hays was the point from which the west and southwest obtained supplies until the Santa Fe railroad was completed to Dodge City. Long trains of heavily-laden wagons were a common sight. Among these were the outfits owned by Otero and Sellar, prominent freighters, who had a large warehouse along the railroad. Bullwhackers were seen often on the streets. One day a party of scientists from the East came to Hays. One member of the party stood gazing, with open mouth, at some object across the street. A bullwhacker noticed him and seized this opportunity to walk up and crack his lash within an inch of the man's spine. The latter jumped into the air, and certain that he had been shot came on the run to his friends to have the ball extracted.[32]

The Cattle Trails

THE Cowboy Era in Kansas and adjoining states began in 1867 when the completion of the Kansas Pacific Railroad to Abilene opened a northern market for Texas' three and a half million cattle. The honor of originating the Kansas and Texas cattle-trails is due to Joseph G. McCoy, an Illinois stock dealer, who was familiar with the need of a market for Texas cattle and conceived the idea of making Abilene the shipping point on the new railroad. The railroad officials were persuaded to build yards in this little town of less than a dozen houses and plans were made to induce the cattlemen to ship their herds from this point. A horseman was dispatched across the prairies for this purpose. He went southwest, crossed the Arkansas near the present site of Wichita and continued on into the Indian Territory. A herd of nearly two thousand cattle, belonging to some Californians, was the first to reach Abilene.

The first shipment, consisting of twenty cars of Texas cattle, was made to Chicago on September 5, 1867. Several stockmen and others joined in an excursion from Springfield, Illinois, to Abilene to celebrate the event. They arrived in the evening where they found large tents, including one for dining purposes, ready for them. A banquet was held that evening, after which speeches were made and wine was served until a late hour at night.[1]

About 35,000 head of cattle arrived in the new shipping point in 1867, 20,000 of which were shipped; the following year the northern drive exceeded 75,000 head; in 1869 the number increased to 150,000.[2]

By 1869 the main trails were well defined. They twisted and turned this way and that to suit the erratic bearings of the streams and to strike convenient camp-grounds. The best known of these was the Chisholm Trail, named for Jesse Chisholm who, a few years earlier, had established a route south from his ranch near the Wichita Indian village, where the City of Wichita now stands, to enable traders to obtain wagon communication with the Indians in the Indian Territory. The Chisholm Trail ran north from Red River Station across the Indian Territory, and entered Kansas near Caldwell. It crossed the Arkansas River at Wichita and continued past the present site of Newton to Abilene. The "Old Shawnee Trail" led from the Red River to Baxter Springs in southeastern Kansas, another northern shipping-point opened about the same time as Abilene, but never so important as a cattle market. In the seventies, the trail through the Creek Nation to Baxter was known as the Okmulkee route. Between the two main trails was the "West Shawnee Trail," which left its namesake near the Canadian River and ended at Junction City. A new trail, known as Cox's Trail or the Ellsworth Cattle Trail, was surveyed to Ellsworth in the spring of 1873. The party, to whom the work of making the survey was entrusted, consisted of William M. Cox, General Live Stock Agent for the

Kansas Pacific Railroad, and four well-known Texas cattle-men. The new route branched off from the old trail at the Pond Creek ranch about half way between Salt Fork of the Arkansas River and Pond Creek, Indian Territory, and ran by way of Kingman and Ellinwood to Ellsworth. It was west of the thickly-settled part of Kansas and was about thirty-five miles shorter than the old trail to Ellsworth. Trails were established to Dodge City and other points in western Kansas, and many herds were driven to Nebraska and other northern and western states and territories.

Trail-driving to Kansas lasted for about two decades, though it was at its height during the first ten years. Definite figures on the northern drives are not available and estimates do not agree. According to Joseph Nimmo, the Government statistician, between five and six millions of cattle were driven north from Texas during the twenty years.[3] The cattle kings of Texas, as well as the small ranchmen, drove their herds to Kansas. In 1870 the Abilene *Chronicle* stated that the bulk of the cattle held in that place were owned by big cattlemen who usually possessed from 5,000 to 10,000 head each. A small drover owned from 100 to 1,000 head.

The Northern Drive

In the early years, one thousand head of cattle was considered a large herd, but in the seventies and eighties, the herds often consisted of five or six thousand cattle. The size of the crew depended on the size of the herd. One or two herders to a hundred head of cattle was the usual rule. The trail-hands were selected with the greatest care. Each cowboy needed from two to six horses. Besides the herders, a trail-boss; a cook; two horse-wranglers who cared for the extra horses; several wagons; pack-mules to carry provisions: and an abundant supply of fire-arms, saddles, lariats, blankets, short-handled whips, bedding, slickers, clothing, and other personal belongings of the riders, made up the outfit.

When everything was ready, the herd was started up the trail. A herd of two thousand cattle would string out a mile or two in length. The width of the line would vary from a few longhorns walking side by side to a group six or eight rods across. Two of the more experienced cowboys riding one on each side, pointed the herd. At regular intervals, other cowboys rode along the flanks, while the least experienced men, called "tenderfeet," brought up the rear of the herd and kept the cattle together as far as possible. Usually the chuck wagon came next, and then the extra horses. The order of march varied at times: the chuck wagon and the extra horses went ahead and made camp before the herd arrived. When the cattle became excited or restless, a cowboy rode ahead and sang a low lullaby, like a mother to her child, to quiet them, for the human voice had a soothing effect on the animals.

A herd composed of longhorns from different ranches was restless the first few days on the trail, and it was necessary for the crew to ride night and day. There was danger that the cattle would break for their regular feeding ground. For the first three or four days, they traveled at the rate of twenty-five to thirty miles a day. There were at least three reasons for doing this. First, the animals would be more easily controlled after they were gotten off their accustomed range; Second, hard driving would tire them out so that they would lie down to rest at night; and Third, it was advisable to break them into driving as soon as possible. The drive was decreased to twelve to fifteen miles a day as soon as it was safe to do so.

At daybreak the herders were aroused by the cook who had breakfast ready. After breakfast the cowboys saddled their horses and commenced the day's work. The herd grazed until about eight o'clock, then traveled until about eleven, when the cattle were permitted to stop and graze or rest until two o'clock. They were again turned into the trail and the line of march was resumed.

The herders made it a point to reach a camping place about five o'clock in the afternoon where a halt was made for the night. The cattle grazed until dusk when the trailhands rounded up the animals for the night, that is they rode round and round, driving or "winding" them into as small a space as possible. Two or more of the men stayed with the cattle in regular relays until morning. In some outfits, one-third of the drivers did guard duty at one time, being relieved at intervals of five hours by other hands who had, in the interim, snatched a few hours of sleep. Occasionally, a thunder storm or other noise in the still hours of the night started a stampede. When this occurred, there was strenuous work, some furious riding, and plenty of hard swearing before the drove was quieted. If the animals became restless or frightened, the herders sang to them, often preventing a stampede.

Much has been written about the men singing and telling stories during the drive up the trail, which has doubtless lead to the notion that the expedition advanced in a care-free manner. The first few nights out, the hands who were not on duty, probably gathered around the camp fire and told tales of adventures with bad men, Indians, or wild cattle. In each outfit, there were usually some good singers who entertained the group with ballads of the plains and trails. Sometimes the entire group joined in the singing and the air rang with the voices of the men singing *Sam Bass, Mustang Grey, The Dying Cowboy, When You and I Were Young Maggie,* and other favorites.

However, trail-driving was far from being a holiday excursion. It was hard, dangerous work and required all hands, the trail-boss, and the cow ponies to do their level best. As the expedition advanced slowly day after day into the boundless prairie, a feeling of loneliness came over most of the men. In the early days, an occasional Indian attack added excitement to the journey, but in the later years, an Indian was seldom seen near the trail. Buffaloes were scarce, so there was little opportunity to break the monotony by taking part in a buffalo-hunt. Thus the trip became painfully dull and tiresome. Each day was so like every other day and each new scene so much a repetition of the scenes already witnessed that being adrift on the prairie was similar to being out at sea—it left a vague, confused impression. After a few days of the march, a spirit of depression was often noticeable in the entire outfit. Only the little cowbirds, which fluttered cheerily around the herd, emitting their guttural chirps, the whole way from the Red River to the Kansas cattle market, seemed to be free from the spell. The men gradually ceased singing around the campfire. Storytelling became a bore. They had little to say and went about largely unmindful of others until some vestige of civilization, perhaps the barking of a dog or the crowing of a rooster, aroused them from their reverie.[4]

When the herds arrived in the vicinity of the town from which they were to be shipped, the trail-boss selected a suitable place for a permanent camp where the cattle could graze and recuperate a month or two before they were marketed. Since the whole country around the cow town was soon filled with longhorns, the drovers found it desirable to arrive as early as possible in the season. Herds were started north as early as March and April. A large part of the cattle reached the cow town by June. Most of the shipping was done late in the summer and in the fall. The vast numbers of cattle in the State at the high point of the season is shown by the following item in the *Saline County Journal* of July 20, 1871:

"The entire country, east, west and south of Salina down to the Arkansas River and Wichita is now filled with Texas cattle. There are not only cattle 'on a thousand hills' but a thousand cattle on one hill and every hill. The bottoms are overflowing with them and the water courses with this great article of traffic. Perhaps not less than 200,000 head are in the state, 60,000 of which are within a day's ride of Salina, and the cry is 'still they come'!"

When Wichita was a leading cattle market, the drovers established camps along the Ninnescah River, Cowskin Creek, and other streams near town where an unusually fine range was found. The country south and west was dotted with cow camps and the hills and valleys were literally black with cattle during the shipping season. The Ninnescah River Station, situated about twenty miles from Wichita, was one of the chief halting places in the State. At this point, the roads to the various grazing grounds branched off from the main trail. Two stores—John Dunscomb's and the Ward McKee Company's —were located at this station and sold supplies to the drovers and their crews.

In 1871 the Wichita City Council designated Douglas Avenue as the thoroughfare for Texas cattle passing through that place. In 1874 a new cattle trail was established which crossed the Arkansas three miles below town, for the purpose of avoiding trouble with the cattle in town and the farmers on the west side. Yards were erected on the west side of the river near the crossing in which the cattle were held over night at such times as the shipping yards were too full. The trail was marked from Cowskin Creek to the ford by a line of red flags bearing the lone star.[5]

A Texas longhorn paid no attention to a man on horseback, but he was a dangerous beast when someone approached him on foot. One day a lad, who was employed by a cattleman near Abilene, went into the lot to feed the stock. A donkey was standing between him and the cattle when he entered the feed-lot. Just then the donkey walked away. A longhorn steer made for the young man who ran and climbed a tree where he remained for two hours before anyone came to his assistance. When longhorns were driven through the streets of a town, cowboys rode ahead and warned everyone to leave the streets. The story is told that a woman in Abilene failed to heed this warning and remained on the street. A steer picked her up on his horns and tossed her into the air. She landed among the marching herd and was trampled under foot. Her body was cut to pieces by the hoofs of the cattle.

The distance from the Red River in northern Texas to the Kansas cow towns was from 300 to 350 miles and the drive was made in 30 or 40 days. The losses sustained during the drives were from five to ten per cent and they were occasioned from death, lameness, thievery, and stampeding. The estimated cost of driving was from $1 to $3 per head.

The drivers were paid $30 to $40 a month, or twice that much if they owned their own horses. The boss-drover received $150 per month. Cow ponies cost $45 each.

When the market was opened in Abilene in 1867, the prices of cattle in Texas were as follows: Yearlings $1 to $2; two-year olds, $3 to $4; three-year olds and cows, $4 to $6; beeves, $7 to $8. There was a prejudice against Texas stock in the northern and eastern markets. Furthermore, a corn crop failure in Ohio, Indiana, and Illinois threw thousands of head on the Chicago market. Early that fall, the price in Abilene was $11 a head for young stock and $17 or $18 for the older animals. In November of that year, because of the congested market, the longhorns were sold in Abilene for $5 and $6 a head. In 1871 the prices in Texas were: Yearlings, $3 to $4; two-year olds, $6 to $7; three-year olds, $8 to $9; four-year olds or beeves, $10 to $18. The prices in Newton that year were: Yearlings $6 to $7; two-year olds, $10 to $12; three-year olds, $16 to $20; four-year olds and beeves, $20 to $26.[6]

Stampedes

"A stampede," says one writer, "is something which baffles description; you must witness it. It is a tempest of horns and tails, a thunder of hoofs, a lighting of wild eyes; I can describe it no better." Some trifling thing often started a stampede. The bark of a coyote, when everything was still at night, was sufficient to stampede a herd. The meeting of a wagon on the trail sometimes excited the cattle. One time a herd of four thousand cattle were being driven up the trail. One of the cowboys opened his tobacco pouch to get a chew. The wind blew a shred or two of the fine-cut tobacco out of his fingers. The tobacco floated away and lodged in the eye of a nearby steer. In a moment, the eye began to smart and the steer began to prance around. Its antics excited others; in a few seconds, the whole herd was surging and dashing about, and stampeded. It was two days before the cattle were completely quieted. Two of the trail-hands were trampled to death and four hundred cattle were lost.

A thunder storm at night usually caused a stampede. The cow men dreaded hail storms when the cattle were sleeping. On one occasion, a hail-stone struck a steer in the eye; he sprang to his feet and tramped on the tails of others. They jumped up; the alarm spread, and before anything could be done, the entire herd was running madly across the prairie.

During a stampede, the cowboys tried to keep the herd together and to get the cattle to milling, that is going around in a circle. With this object in view, they pressed the leaders to the right and gradually forced the column of frantic cattle to run in a circle. When this was done, the first step toward controlling them was accomplished. Quite often the long-horns would run miles at night, and mingle with other herds, before they were stopped. Next morning the cowmen spent several hours separating the herds. Instances are on record where the cowboys were obliged to ride a distance of over a hundred miles before they got the herd under control and then found that they were not more than twenty-five miles from where the stampede started.[7]

In the seventies, public corrals were common along the trails in Texas. They were built of logs and were round so that, when the cattle became excited, the men could ride around them, and by yelling and shaking blankets and slickers could start the animals milling. Occasionally the beasts would bolt through the side of the corral as though it was made of paper and run across country with the men in hot pursuit.

High Water

The river crossings were sources of trouble, especially when heavy rains caused the river to rise. The cattle were usually taken across in groups of twenty-five or thirty. The cowboys stripped off their clothing, and one swam his horse ahead of the cattle while others rode along the sides and in the rear. Sometimes a whole herd could be driven across without any trouble. At other times, the cattle would reach the opposite shore when the sudden appearance of a rabbit or other moving object would frighten one of the lead-steers and he would turn back. In a moment, the whole group would be swimming wildly round and round in the middle of the stream. In some instances, the drovers had to work for hours to break up the mill. In doing this, it was necessary for the cowboys to leave their horses and swim among the cattle, and possibly get on the horns or backs of the animals. The cattle frequently drifted down the stream quite a distance before the mill was broken. The cottonwood trees on the shore were usually loaded with hornets' nests. When the drovers and cattle passed under the trees, the hornets would drop on them, stinging man and beast. The animals, unable to stand the stings, usually ceased milling and made for the shore. Often times, the crew worked for days to get a herd of four or five thousand head of cattle across a stream and many a brave cow-puncher was drowned during the process.

The crossing of the Arkansas near Wichita was the scene of several unpleasant incidents which are related in the literature of the trails. A near-tragedy occurred at this ford in June, 1872.

A cattleman was getting a herd across when the water was up to the swimming point. The banks were crowded with spectators. The strange song of the herders, the splash, whoop and bellow, riders and longhorns mingled in the rushing current of the river, made a scene both wild and interesting. During the melee, a chivalric deed of heroism was performed that thrilled all present. A herder's horse went under with him, and as the both arose, the horse kicked its rider who was struggling nearby with the current. The man sank, came up, and went down the second time when a stranger standing on the shore divested himself of coat, vest, and hat, and while the stupefied crowd stood in silence on the banks, he plunged into the turbulent Arkansas, swam out toward the drowning man, grasped him in his last struggle, and after a desperate effort to keep the herder from drowning him, succeeded in getting into shallow water, then to the shore. It took sometime to resuscitate the nearly-drowned cowboy. Meantime, the hero resumed his clothing, and quietly mingling with the spectators, was lost from view so his name was not known.[8]

The cattlemen were also inconvenienced by owners of ferries obstructing the fords. This did not occur often. It was not for the interest of these men to block the progress of the cattle as they were constantly employed by the drovers to assist in driving the herds across the streams and were paid for their work.[9]

Indians

In the early days of trail-driving, the Indians frequently killed or drove off a number of the cattle or committed some other form of deviltry when the herds were driven through the Indian Territory. A band of red skins would come to the drovers and demand a certain number of cattle on the threat that they would stampede the herd. If the whites felt strong enough, they put up a fight and drove the Indians off or compromised by giving them a few head. Sometimes the Indians killed or drove off as high as ten per cent of the herd. There are instances on record when a herd was stampeded and the cowboys killed. In the seventies, some of the tribes levied a tax on all cattle driven through their territory. Drovers who refused to pay this tribute, had trouble on their hands, and some real fights ensued.

The cattlemen undertook the long drive with the knowledge that trouble could be expected north of the Red River. They prepared for it by taking along a supply of firearms and ammunition and by hiring cowboys who would fight. The crews usually contained some of the hardest characters on the frontier. Some of the drovers employed professional gunmen to accompany their outfit as an extra precaution.

The vigorous defense of the cattlemen caused the Indians to desist from their raids on the herds. They learned that the cowboys were ready for them and meant business. In the late seventies and eighties, Indians were seldom seen along the trails. The only regular annoyance from the red skins was their exaction of toll for the passage of the cattle through their domain.

The Creek Indians were friendlier toward the Texas men than were some of the other tribes. The Council of the Creek Nation convened March 6, 1871, and passed a bill providing for the grazing and herding of stock in transit through the Creek territory. The bill provided that the drover should have the right to graze and herd his stock in any part of the Creek domain during the cattle season of the year ending November 30; gave access to any part of the nation without reservation of district; gave sufficient wood for camping purposes; and in consideration for this required the payment of a license of twenty-five cents a head per month to the Creek Nation.

The Creek Indians, along the Okmulkee route, manifested a most friendly feeling toward the drovers. In the spring of 1871, they built a new road through their Nation by way of the Okmulkee route. A tax of 27½ cents per head was levied on cattle going by this route to Baxter.[10]

Outlaws

The stealing of cattle and other valuables was not confined to the Indians. White men also engaged in this nefarious occupation.

Early in 1870, a man named Harney came to Marion in pursuit of sixty head of cattle that had been stolen from him. He met the thieves on the way and thought that William Martin, known as "Hurricane Bill," was at the head of the gang. Afraid to attack them alone, he came to Marion for help. A posse struck the trail, and on coming in sight of the outfit, defeated the thieves and recovered the cattle.

In June, 1871, a man on his way to Texas to buy cattle was murdered near Columbus, Cherokee County, by another man. Both men were on horseback. While the murderer was rifling the pockets of his victim, he was seized by some men, who

had watched the proceedings from an adjoining field, and was
hung on the spot.

A month later drovers were attacked and their cattle maltreated near Schuyler, Nebraska. Sixteen armed men met the
son of Judge Fant, the earliest and warmest advocate of that
town's claims as a cattle market, who had one of the droves in
his immediate charge; and tried, without shooting, to frighten
him to a distance and to stampede his drove with the intention
of stealing as many cattle as possible. They failed to accom-
plish their purpose. About the same time, the herds belonging
to Smith Brothers arrived at Schuyler in a bad condition. The
owners reported that the cattle had been fearfully maltreated
in their progress up the Little Blue.[11]

Cattleman Versus Farmer

The Texas cattle trade had scarcely gotten under way
when the settlers began to oppose the northern drive. The
farmers residing near the cattle trails and cow towns continued their opposition throughout the entire period. As the set-
tlements advanced westward, the cattlemen found it advisable to lay out new trails, skirting the settled region, and to
open new markets farther west.

The fear that Spanish or Texas fever would spread among
the native cattle was the chief cause of the hostility. Furthermore, the Texas cattle, in some instances, broke down the
farmer's fences and destroyed his crops or were driven promiscuously over his land. The settlers saw a great deal of loss
and very little profit coming out of the Texas cattle trade.

Marked opposition was early in evidence among the farmers residing near Abilene. They organized a company for the
purpose of stampeding every drove of cattle that came into
the county. With this end in view, they elected the most intelligent of their number as their captain and bound themselves

by a solemn pledge to keep up their opposition until the Texas cattle trade was abandoned.

Open hostility was averted by a diplomatic move on the part of Joseph G. McCoy and others. They sent word to the Captain to call as many of his company as possible to a meeting at his cabin on a designated evening, at which time the cattle trade would be discussed. On the appointed evening, several Texas drovers accompanied McCoy to the Captain's cabin where a few settlers had gathered. By a previous arrangement, McCoy addressed the farmers, pointing out the financial advantages of the cattle trade for them and their community. While he was making this talk, the drovers went among the farmers bartering for butter, eggs, potatoes, onions, oats, corn, and such other products as they could use, paying from one-fourth to double the price asked by the settlers.

At the conclusion of the meeting, the Captain said that he had gotten a "sight" of the cattle trade that was new and convincing to him. "And, gentlemen," said he, "if I can make any money out of this cattle trade, I am not afraid of 'Spanish fever'; but if I can't make any money out of this cattle trade, then I am d——d afraid of 'Spanish fever.'" The organization dissolved without any further trouble.[12]

The hostility to the cattle traffic gained ground in the next few years, despite the efforts of McCoy and other friends of the trade. Leading men in Abilene joined the hostile farmers in this opposition. In February, 1872, a notification to the drovers not to come back to Abilene with their herds was published and was circulated in Texas. Friends of the trade tried to counteract the effects of the circular. Petitions were circulated and signed, asking the cattlemen to return, but it was too late. The trade went to Ellsworth and other markets.

Shortly after the cattle trade shifted to Ellsworth, opposition developed in that county. In March, 1872, a meeting was held at the Thompson Creek school house, the object of which was to formulate plans for preventing the spread of disease among the native cattle and to stop the driving of cattle promiscuously over the farms as had been done the previous year. With that purpose in view, those present formed the Ellsworth County Farmers Protective Society.[13]

A decade later homesteaders came into southwestern Kansas in large numbers and the struggle began in that section between the cattleman and the farmer, which continued for several years when the latter won the contest. At the start, the cattlemen tried to discourage the homesteader by such remarks as the following: "Say, let us tell you something. It never rains out there and you will starve to death. Dodge City is as far west as civilization will ever go, and that place is hardly fit for a civilized man with a family." [14]

By the spring of 1885, the settlers were coming in so fast that they broke up the range. At this time a Garden City newspaper reported that the stockmen were setting the prairie on fire for the purpose of driving out the farmers. The cowboys of the big X Y ranch, becoming intoxicated in Garden City, would race their horses past the sod houses of humble homes of the settlers, emit blood-curdling yells, and fire off their revolvers in order to scare the women and children and intimidate the settlers into leaving.[15] The terrible blizzard of 1886, which destroyed thousands of head of livestock on the open range and caused heavy financial losses to the owners, was the final blow to the range cattle industry. The cattlemen gave up the fight and the farmers remained in possession of the land.

The Kansas Cow Towns

THERE were a score of shipping points in Kansas for Texas cattle. Of these, only four or five have gained a national reputation as wild and woolly cow towns. Abilene is the oldest, and in some respects, the most widely known of this group. Its fame as a longhorn metropolis rests largely on the numerous stories of wild night life and gun battles. These stories are a part of the folk-say of the community and form an important chapter in the lore of the plains. To us, who are removed from the misery and tragedy of it all, there is something romantic about the boisterous night-life in the saloons, gambling houses, and dance halls; something fascinating about drunken brawls over cards and painted women; and thrilling about famous gun-fighters snuffing the life out of equally famous gun fighters with six-shooters.

Abilene[1]

The town of Abilene was laid out in 1860 on land belonging to C. H. Thompson who had moved into the county from Leavenworth in the spring of that year. The name of the future cattle market was Biblical in origin, though this never would have been suspected after the cattle trade reached its height. When a name for the town was under consideration, Thompson asked Tim Hersey, his neighbor on the other side of Mud Creek, to suggest a name.

"No," was the reply, "let my wife do it; she is a great reader."

Mrs. Hersey knew her Bible from cover to cover. When the question of a name was referred to her, she turned to the third chapter of Luke, first Verse, and read, "Now in the fifteenth year of the reign of Tiberius Caesar, Pontius Pilate being governor of Judea . . . and Lysanias tetrarch of Abilene." Looking up, she said,

"Call the town 'Abilene.' It means 'City of the Plains,' and that exactly describes the location."

The growth of Abilene was slow during the first few years. About the only advertisement the young town had was Tim Hersey's log boarding-house and crude stable known as station number 2 on the Butterfield Overland Despatch established between Atchison and Denver in 1865 by David Butterfield and later taken over by Ben Holladay, the Overland Stage King. The town, in 1867, was described as a "small, dead place consisting of about a dozen log huts, low, small, rude affairs, four-fifths of which were covered with dirt for roofing."

In 1867 the Kansas Pacific Railroad was building west from Kansas City and was completed to Abilene in March; to Ellsworth in July; and to Hays in October. Joseph G. McCoy of Springfield, Illinois, one of three brothers who had engaged in the buying and shipping of cattle for some years, conceived the idea of establishing a cattle trail and a shipping station for Texas longhorns at some point on the Kansas Pacific Railroad. Accordingly, the Chisholm Trail was laid out and Abilene was selected as the railway shipping point.

As soon as the cattle market was opened in Abilene, a remarkable change took place. The log huts gave way to frame buildings. Numerous business houses were erected and the town took on an air of prosperity. In 1870 there were four hotels, ten boarding-houses, five dry goods and clothing stores, nine or ten saloons, and other business establishments. The majority of the buildings were one-story frame structures, though some had two or even three stories. The first buildings constructed of other than wood were the jail and court house erected in 1870. The side walks were of wood and presented an irregular appearance to the eye.

Texas Abilene was south of the railroad. Lone Star life began on First Street (Texas Street) near Mulberry, about two blocks east of the cattle crossing on Mud Creek, ran east on First Street to Cedar, north on Cedar to A Street (Railroad Street), then east on A Street. Most of the buildings, which were the scene of stories in trail days, were located on the above-mentioned streets. H. H. Hazlett's Drovers' Outfitting Store was on the southwest corner of Mulberry and First Streets. In the block east: The Planters Hotel; Bull's Head Saloon opened by Phil Coe and Ben Thompson in 1871; the Applejack and Old Fruit Saloons; and Jac. (Jake) Karatofsky's Great Western Store on the corner of Cedar. Karatofsky, a young Russian Jew, kept a stock of dry goods, clothing, and other merchandise in his store.

Around the corner on Cedar, and facing the west, was the

Alamo Saloon, Wild Bill Hickok's headquarters when he was City Marshal. The entrance to this saloon consisted of three sets of double-glass doors extending across the front.

On A Street, facing the railroad, were four saloons in a row; the Novelty Theatre opened in July, 1871, with an experienced manager and actor in charge; and the Gulf House, a two-story hotel. This building still stands. Another story has been added and the name changed to National Hotel. Up the street were Mayor Henry's office; and the Drover's Cottage which was built by McCoy in the fall of 1867 and opened to the public in 1868 under the management of J. W. and Louisa Gore of St. Louis. This hotel was popular with the cattlemen and many of the leading drovers, speculators, and gamblers patronized it. Major M. B. George, a cattleman, purchased the property in 1870 and enlarged the building. The following year it was described as one of the largest hotels in the West—three stories high; 100 rooms; new laundry; and new barn with room for 100 horses and 50 carriages.

The stockyards were located along the railroad at the east edge of town and covered several acres of ground. The yards were enlarged and the side track lengthened in 1869.

In the early days the tough district was a mile and a half north of town and consisted of twenty-five or thirty one-story frame houses with ten to twenty rooms in each house. The buildings were suppressed in 1870. After McCoy became Mayor in the spring of '71, a tract of land at the east edge of town was procured for these houses. The district was then dubbed "McCoy's Addition" by some; "Devil's Half-acre" by others.

Abilene was one of the liveliest towns in the West after it became a cattle market. Hundreds of drovers, cattle buyers, commission men, and speculators made it their headquarters. A motley crew of bad characters flocked there to prey on the cattlemen. The local paper stated that at one time during the season of '71 there was a "larger number of cut-throats and desperadoes in Abilene than in any other town of its size on the continent. Most of them were from Kansas City, St. Louis, New Orleans, Chicago and from the mountains." Wes Hardin, who could boast of forty notches on his gun and saw a lot of wickedness, spent some time in Abilene that season and says of it:

"I have seen many fast towns, but I think Abilene beats them all. The town was filled with sporting men and women, gamblers, cowboys, desperadoes and the like. It was well supplied with barrooms, hotels, barbershops and gambling houses, and everything was open."

Little attempt was made to control the disorder and curb the lawlessness the first two seasons. There was no municipal government, no jail, and no effective police system. The town was wide open. Everyone had a right to be drunk, to gamble when and where he pleased, and to carry and discharge firearms. Wild shouts and pistol shots kept the orderly citizens in dread of their lives day and night those two years.

In September, 1869, the town was incorporated as a third class city. The Court appointed a Board of Trustees consisting of five members; namely, James B. Shane and Theodore C. Henry, partners in the real estate business; Thomas Sheran, a grocer, and one-time Sheriff of the county; and Tim Hersey and J. G. McCoy, mentioned above. The Board chose Henry as Chairman which, in effect, made him mayor of the city. The close of the shipping season was so near at hand that little was done that fall toward curbing the violence. The next spring the Board was re-organized; C. H. Lebold, a young real estate man, and Dr. H. C. Brown took the places of Messrs. Hersey and McCoy. Washburne Fancher, a youthful school master, was appointed secretary of the Board. The saloons were licensed, houses of ill-fame regulated, and the more flagrant crimes were punished. An ordinance providing that no one would be allowed to carry firearms in town was passed. This ordinance was printed and posted.

The cowmen were determined that these ordinances, especially the deadly-weapon ordinance, should not be enforced. They shot to pieces the copies that were posted.

The new government decided to employ a City Marshal. Several local men applied. One man after another was appointed, but failed to restrain the lawless element. The construction of a stone jail was begun. When the walls were almost up, the cowboys demolished the structure. The building was then erected under the protection of a guard. The first prisoner was a negro cook from one of the cattle camps on Mud Creek who had been arrested for shooting at the street lamps. His camp companions frightened away the peace officers, blew off the jail lock, and released him. Then they directed the business houses to close, in some instances riding into the stores on horseback to enforce their mandate. A squad of horsemen galloped up Railroad Street, shot the Mayor's office full of holes, and rode on to the stockyards. A posse of armed citizens started after the disorderly group, but captured only a few.

Other marshals were tried and failed. Finally, the Mayor asked the chief of police of St. Louis to send out two competent men. In response to this request, two highly-recommended soldiers came to Abilene to look into the situation. The cowmen, aware of their mission, contrived all sorts of devilish devices and turned them loose the day these "tenderfeet" arrived. The two men went home on the midnight train.

During this period of disorder, strange as it may seem, very few people were killed. The Federal Census enumerator in July, 1870, did not report anyone killed with firearms in Dickinson County during the year ending June 1st; however, he failed to say how many were scared almost to death by that type of weapon during those twelve months. During the same period, a policeman and two prostitutes were killed in Ellsworth and three men were shot to death in street brawls in Hays.

The city fathers, at their wits end to know what to do, decided to employ Thomas J. Smith who was one of the first applicants for the position, having come down from Kit Carson, Colorado, when he learned that a marshal was wanted.

Tom Smith was a fine looking, broad shouldered, athletic man about five feet eleven inches in height, who tipped the scales at 170 pounds, stood erect, had grayish blue eyes, auburn hair, and light mustache. He was gentle in manners, low toned in speech, deferential in the presence of official superiors, and brave beyond question. He deserves first place in the gallery of frontier marshals.

Smith was born of Irish parents in New York in 1830. Little is known of his early life beyond the fact that he received a fair education and was reared in the Catholic faith. When the Union Pacific was building across Nebraska in 1867, he was employed in various capacities in the construction of the railroad. The following year he was engaged with a large contracting firm whose headquarters were at Bear River City, Wyoming, and took part in the Bear River riot, a bloody frontier fight. Smith received severe wounds in this engagement, and by the time he recovered the construction gang had abandoned Bear River City and moved on. His conduct had been such in the riot that he was chosen marshal of the next town and the next as one town was abandoned and another located along the right of way.

The Board of Trustees of Abilene met late in the afternoon of June 4 for the purpose of re-organizing the police force. A motion was passed employing Tom Smith as Chief of Police for one month at a salary of $150 per month. The "old police" were requested to resign and provision was made that, when any person was convicted, the policeman making the arrest should receive the sum of $2.00.

The new Marshal did not subdue the town singlehanded as is sometimes said. The day he was appointed a motion was passed providing that "Mr. Smith select a man to assist him." Nine days later the Board met again. Mr. Robbins was introduced. He proposed to act as policeman at a salary of $150 per month, and on motion of Doctor Brown he was employed. The municipal records are incomplete and fail to show how long Robbins served or how many other men were on the police that season. It appears certain that James H. McDonald was put on the force late in the summer or in the fall and was to see some strenuous and bloody service. McDonald was listed as a laborer before he became a policeman. He was a native of Canada, twenty-one years old, tall, of medium weight for his height, and had a fair complexion. It is said that McDonald held a commission as Deputy United States Marshal while he was a peace officer in Abilene.

Tom Smith's first maneuver in his campaign on lawlessness was to enforce the ordinance against gun-toting. He enlisted the help of the businessmen and persuaded the proprietors of the hotels to use their safes as depositories for the pistols of drovers and other guests. The Texas cattle owners, as well as the local merchants, saw the wisdom of his plan and gave it their support. New copies of the ordinance were printed and posted.

The Marshal rode on horseback and used his fists to enforce the ordinance—two innovations on the frontier. Other peace officers had walked and had depended on six-shooters. He had a double purpose in riding. First, as he marched "Silverheels," his favorite gray, down the middle of the street he could more easily see anyone waiting ahead of him or approaching from behind. Second, it is more difficult to shoot a man who is riding than one on foot. The cowmen relied on guns and were at a decided disadvantage in a pugilistic contest.

On a Saturday night, soon after Smith assumed the duties of his office, a rowdy styled "Big Hank" challenged his authority. Big Hank had defied former marshals and boasted that no officer could disarm him. Wearing a belted six-shooter, he approached the Marshal and asked,

"Are you the man who proposes to run this town?"

"I am employed as Marshal and shall try to maintain order and enforce the law," Smith replied.

"What are you going to do about that gun ordinance?"

"See that it is obeyed; I must trouble you to hand me yours."

With an oath, the cowboy refused to give up his arms. In a calm tone of voice, the Marshal repeated the demand. This brought forth more profanity and abuse. Smith sprang forward and landed a terrific blow on Big Hank's jaw. Then he took the ruffian's pistol from him and ordered him to leave town, a command that was quickly obeyed.

The news of this encounter traveled on wings and before midnight it was the leading topic of conversation in the cattle camps around Abilene. The cowboys discussed the episode from every angle and debated pro and con this unique method of law enforcement. In a camp on a branch of Chapman Creek northeast of town, a wager was made by Wyoming Frank, a big burly fellow, that he could go to Abilene and defy the Marshal. Next morning Frank was on hand to carry out his boast. Smith was late in appearing. Finally, he came down the middle of the street and Frank went out to meet him. As he approached the Marshal, he began talking insolently with the idea of involving him in a quarrel as an excuse for refusing to surrender the guns which he purposely displayed. Aware of the man's purpose, the officer quietly asked him to hand over his pistol. Frank refused the demand and began backing as

Smith advanced, calling for the gun. The former continued to back, maneuvering for time and space in which to draw his six-shooter, but the latter's close-reach prevented him from doing so. Finally the cowman backed into a saloon, followed by the Marshal, and stopped in the center of the room where a crowd gathered around the two. Again Smith courteously demanded the gun. An insulting oath was the reply. The Marshal vaulted and with a double blow sent Wyoming Frank to the floor and beat him with the unbelted pistol. Then standing over him, Smith said,

"I give you five minutes to get out of this town, and don't you ever let me set eyes on you again."

The witnesses stood speechless for a moment; the proprietor was the first to break the silence. Stepping from behind the bar, he said,

"That was the nerviest act I ever saw. You did your duty, and that coward got what he deserved. Here is my gun. I reckon I'll not need it so long as you are Marshal of this town."

Every man in the room now pressed forward, proffering the Marshal his pistol and complimenting him. He thanked them and said,

"Hand your guns to the bartender to keep until you want to go out to camp."

Tom Smith had conquered the town. Thereafter most visitors obeyed the deadly-weapon ordinance. There was drunkenness, an occasional fight, and late in the summer a man was killed in one of the dens of infamy northwest of town. The Marshal had done his work so well that the Trustees, on August 9, voted to increase his salary to $225 per month to date from July 4, the beginning of his second month of service.

At this time there lived in a dugout near Chapman Creek, ten or twelve miles northeast of Abilene, a Scotchman named Andrew McConnell. He was a good-sized man, thirty-five years old, and had blue eyes, light brown hair, and a light full beard. His friend Moses Miles owned a nearby farm. Miles was a native of Massachusetts, the same age as McConnell, but of a heavier build, and had dark hair, and a swarthy complexion. One or both had lived in Colorado for ten or twelve years and are said to have left a shady record there. John Shea, a thirty-six year old Irishman, resided on another farm in the Chapman Creek neighborhood with his wife and two small children.

On Sunday afternoon, October 23, McConnell was out hunting deer, and on returning found Shea driving cattle across his land. The cattle had destroyed some of his corn. According to the most reliable contemporary reports, words passed between the two men. The Irishman drew his revolver and snapped it twice at the Scotchman. As he was cocking his pistol for a third attempt, McConnell shot him through the heart. The Scotchman went for a doctor and afterwards gave himself up to the authorities. He was released when Miles testified that the act was done in self defense.

Some of the neighbors had a different idea of the affair and told the officers unmistakable circumstances made it appear that Shea was not the aggressor. Complaint was made by John Ryan before E. Barber, Justice of the Peace, and a warrant was issued for the arrest of the Scotchman. Joseph Cramer, Sheriff of the County, or one of his deputies, tried to serve the warrant, but was driven off the place and came to Abilene for help. Tom Smith, who was a Deputy United States Marshal as well as Chief of Police, volunteered to make the arrest. With Officer McDonald, Smith, on Wednesday afternoon, November 2, went to McConnell's dugout to make the arrest. On reaching the dugout, they found McConnell and Miles there. Smith went in and told McConnell that he had a warrant for his arrest, whereupon the Scotchman shot him through the right lung. Smith also fired wounding Mc-

Connell. The two men, being close together, grappled. Meantime, a vigorous fusillade took place between McDonald and Miles; the latter was wounded, but succeeded in driving the former off the place. At this time Smith brought McConnell outside the door of the dugout. Miles, rid of McDonald, struck the Marshal on the head with his gun felling him to the ground. The two men dragged him about ten yards from the dugout; then Miles seized an axe and chopped Smith's head nearly off from his body.

At this stage of the tragedy, McDonald, leaving his horse where it was tied, ran to the nearest claim, a half-mile or more west, mounted a pony and rode back to Abilene for assistance. In a few minutes, a posse was raised who repaired to the scene of the murder. McConnell and Miles had fled. They reached Junction City that evening, then started up the Republican River Valley toward Clay Center, intending to escape to the mountains in Colorado.

Judge C. C. Kuney and James Gainsford, a butcher by trade, who were with the posse, started in pursuit and continued on the trail, traveling almost day and night, until the men were captured. They lost track of the fugitives on the Republican River and went nearly one hundred miles out of the way. They found the trail again at Milford and continued on to Clay Center where they were joined by Sheriff Rodman and others. The party renewed the pursuit at 3 o'clock Saturday morning and about sunrise they came to a farm house fifteen miles northwest of town. Before reaching the place, they learned that two men had stopped there the previous evening. As they approached the house, Gainsford went toward the rear door while Judge Kuney entered the house at the front door. The former met Miles back of the house. The latter came upon McConnell immediately upon entering the house. Both men surrendered without offering resistance.

The officers brought their prisoners to Abilene on the Sunday morning train. From a telegraphic dispatch, sent from Junction City, Abilene folk learned that they had been captured and a large crowd gathered at the depot when the train arrived. Threats of lynching were made, but the officers hurried the prisoners to a room on the second floor of the court house where they were securely guarded until Monday when they were brought before the Justice of the Peace, E. Barber, for a preliminary hearing. They waived an examination and were remanded to the custody of Sheriff Cramer. The District Court was in session in Abilene at that time. A day and a half was consumed in trying to impanel a jury. Three special venues were exhausted without securing the requisite number of jurors. Thereupon the court granted a change of venue to Riley County, and the prisoners were conveyed to the Manhattan jail. The trial took place at the March term. Both men were found guilty and served terms in the penitentiary.

The Texas cattle trade in Abilene reached its height in 1871. It is estimated that six hundred thousand cattle arrived in western Kansas during the season. For miles north, south and west of Abilene one was scarcely out of sight of a herd. The drive to Abilene started from Texas in March, the herds ranging in size from 1,000 to 25,000 cattle each. On April 6, the Abilene *Chronicle* estimated that not less than 90,000 longhorns were on their way to Abilene. On May 25 the local paper reported that between twenty-seven and thirty thousand cattle were in the vicinity. As the season advanced, a person standing on top of a commanding hill could often see from thirty to fifty thousand head at one view. It is said that there were more than five thousand cowboys in and around Abilene.

The rough element came in larger numbers than usual that season. The local paper stated that at one time during the season there was a "larger number of cut-throats and desperadoes in Abilene than in any other town of its size on the continent."

In the spring Ben Thompson arrived in town. His brother Billy was there off and on during the season. They were among the best known gunmen in the Old West. Bat Masterson once said that the "very name of Ben Thompson was enough to cause the general run of 'man killers,' even those who had never seen him, to seek safety in flight." Ben is the most enigmatic character in Kansas cow town history. He has been rated all the way from a "killer" to a "fine man."

Ben was born in Nova Scotia of English parents in 1844 and spent his boyhood days in Austin, Texas, where he learned the printer's trade on the *Southern Intelligencer*. He was five feet, nine inches tall, of rather swarthy complexion, and blue eyes; stood real straight, making an attractive figure on foot or horseback. He was fastidious about his clothing and personal appearance—not a hair on his head could be out of place. He was generous, loyal to his friends, and a likeable fellow, making friends among people of wealth and influence who helped him out of numerous tight places. Major W. M. Walton, Ben's lawyer biographer, tells how officers and privates assisted him during his stormy term of service in the Confederate army and mentions numerous big cattle men as his friends. Eddie Foy, the comedian, says that Bat Masterson was one of Ben's friends in Dodge City. It is told on good authority that Masterson risked his life and reputation to get Bill out of trouble in Nebraska one time because of his friendship for Ben. Sheriff Whitney is listed among Ben's friends in Ellsworth. Thompson left a good record in Abilene. When the writer asked the older residents of Abilene and Ellsworth, who knew Ben Thompson, for an estimate they spoke highly of him.

One night in Ellsworth Ben got drunk and disturbed the peace. One who has read recent Thompson stories would expect him to terrorize the town and kill at least one peace officer before he sobered up and settled down to a normal life. He did nothing of the kind. The next morning he appeared in Judge Osborne's police court, entered a complaint against himself, and paid his fine.

Thompson's biography reads like fiction. He was in one scrape after another but always escaped. He took his first human life when, as a lad working at the printer's trade in New Orleans, he fought a duel with a Frenchman who had made ungentlemanly remarks to a girl. Friends helped him escape. When the Civil War began, he enlisted in the Confederate army and was a constant trouble maker. After the war he served a two year term in prison for shooting a man. He was released in 1870 and the next spring came to Abilene. He arrived without much money, but gambled and won largely, quitting with nearly $2,600 in his pocket which he decided to invest in a saloon.

Billy Thompson was four years younger than Ben. He resembled his brother in complexion, erect form, attractive appearance, and friendly manner, but was taller and more slender, and had brown hair and gray eyes. Bill appears to have had less self-control than his brother, getting into trouble more often. The old timers do not have much use for Bill.

About the time Ben Thompson won the huge stakes at cards, his old friend Phil Coe of Austin arrived in town. Coe is described as a fine looking man over six feet four inches tall, with brown full beard and mustache. He served for a time in the Confederate army. After the war he drifted from place to place eventually coming to Abilene, and brought some thousands of dollars with him.

Coe and Thompson combined their resources and opened the Bull's Head Saloon on Texas Street. They purchased the most expensive equipment; their faro bank was said to have been the best that money could buy. Whether or not this venture was profitable is uncertain. Most writers accept the statement of Ben's biographer that "a gold mine could not have been more profitable." It is a matter of record, however, that the City Council, at a meeting in July, permitted the transfer of Phil Coe's license to Tom Sheran, an Abilene business man. About this time Ben Thompson went to Kansas City, his biographer says, to bring his family to Abilene, and Coe appears to have devoted his efforts to gambling.

In the charter election that spring, J. G. McCoy was elected Mayor and five substantial citizens were elected to the Council: G. S. Brinkman, S. A. Burroughs, Dr. L. Boudinot, Samuel Carpenter, and W. H. Eicholtz.

Before the cattle season opened, the municipal authorities prepared to fend off trouble. The Mayor wanted J. B (Wild Bill) Hickok for City Marshal. On April 15 the Council unanimously confirmed the appointment. He received a salary of $150 per month and twenty-five percent of the fines. Wild Bill was probably the best known gunman in the Old West when he became Marshal of Abilene. After serving in the Border and Civil Wars, he became a guide, scout, and Indian fighter on the frontier; and for a time was peace officer in Hays, in which capacity Dame Rumor said that he killed at least twelve men and wounded and maimed whole regiments and battalions, whereas the total number of victims of his pistols did not exceed three. The most authentic is the killing of Samuel Strangham or Strawhan (later spelled Strawhorn).

In June, Thomas Carson, James Gainsford, and James H. McDonald were appointed on the police force, the latter two at the unanimous request of the Council. Tom Carson was a nephew of Kit Carson. The fact that he was the nephew of a famous uncle undoubtedly enhanced his prestige as a gunfighter. He served for almost two months as Wild Bill's first deputy and then went to Newton, the "roarin' cowtown" that had sprung up over night on the Santa Fe railroad, where he was employed as Marshal. The part played by McDonald and Gainsford at the time of the murder of Marshal Tom Smith has been told. After Smith's death, a group of citizens petitioned the City Council to appoint McDonald to the office of City Marshal, but the petition was not acted on. The next spring Mayor McCoy appointed McDonald to the office of Street Commissioner. Gainsford received not only fame, but also one hundred dollars for his part in the capture of Smith's murderers. He was also Deputy United States Marshal.

One of Wild Bill's first duties was to require a refractory councilman to attend a council meeting. At the spring election, the licensing of saloons was a leading issue. Two councilmen ran on a $100 license platform; two were elected as $200 men; and one member, Mr. X we shall call him, was a prohibitory or $500 license man. Later a proposal was made to run the city government entirely by license fees and Mr. X switched over to the $100 group. The Council adjourned before the question was settled.

On the evening of the adjourned meeting, Mr. X was absent, but a quorum being present the bill was passed with an amendment fixing the license fee at $200. The two $100 councilmen tendered their resignation. On May 8 the Council met with all members present. The resignations were accepted and the two members left the chamber. Mr. X went also, leaving the Council without a quorum. On the motion of Mr. Brinkman, Wild Bill was instructed to compel Mr. X to return, which order was executed; but as soon as the dissatisfied member entered the room he left it again, going to his law office. The Marshal was again instructed to bring him back. Bill went to the Councilman's office and made known his errand; but the man was defiant so the Marshal threw him over his shoulder, carried him to the council chamber, dumped him into a chair and sat down beside him. The Council proceeded with the scheduled business.

Wild Bill ruled with an iron hand and kept the tough element well within control. In addition to the usual police duties, the city fathers assigned special tasks to him from time to time. He was instructed to close all dance houses and put a stop to the vending of intoxicants in the McCoy addition; to close all lead and brace gambling games and arrest the cappers for these games; to oust the fair Cyprians from the Abilene House; and near the close of the season, to suppress all dance houses and notify all prostitutes and gamblers to come forward and pay their fines. The authorities objected to the sign on the front of the Bull's Head Saloon and instructed Wild Bill to see that it was changed. He notified Coe and Thompson to change it or take it down. As they did not do either, Bill sent up some painters who materially altered the sign.

The Clements boys, Wes Hardin, and William Chorn (written Billy Coran by the Texans), hired out that spring to drive longhorns up the trail. They started for Abilene about March 1 and arrived on the North Cottonwood in May where they went into camp about forty miles south of Abilene. Chorn, a popular young man twenty-two years old, remained on the Cottonwood as boss-herder in Colonel Wheeler's outfit. Hardin and the Clements brothers spent much of their time in Abilene where Wes took part in a number of escapades and had to flee, going to the North Cottonwood.

On July 5, Billy Chorn was killed in a treacherous manner by a Mexican herder named Bideno. He told the Mexican to go to another herd. Bideno refused, and slipping up behind his boss, killed him. The Mexican fled southward on a swift horse. Chorn's body was brought to Abilene. The funeral, said to have been the largest in Abilene up to that time, was held at the Drover's Cottage.

Prominent cowmen urged Wes to follow the murderer, which he consented to do if they would get a warrant from Abilene. They obtained the warrant and Wes was appointed

Deputy Sheriff. Early next morning, he and Jim Rodgers started in pursuit of the Mexican, hoping to overtake him before he reached the Nation. At Newton they were joined by Chorn's brother, who bossed a herd near that place, and by Hugh Anderson of Salado, Texas, who was leader in a bloody gun-battle in Newton a month later. After pursuing Bideno for two hundred miles, they caught up with him at Bluff, a town of about fifty houses near the Kansas line. Wes and Anderson found the Mexican in a restaurant seated at a table. Instead of surrendering, Bideno drew his pistol. Hardin fired across the table, killing him instantly. The four cowmen returned to Abilene where Wes discovered that he was a hero. He received a shower of congratulations and a sprinkling of ten and twenty dollar bills. Wealthy cattlemen also made up a purse of six hundred dollars and presented it to him.

Hardin tells an amusing incident which occurred a few days later. He and Gip Clements had retired for the night in the American Hotel located on Cedar below Texas Street, when he heard a man unlock the door and slip into the room. Wes fired at the man who ran, taking Hardin's trousers with him. The shooting aroused the police who drove up in a hack. Wes, minus his trousers, waited until they went inside the hotel; then he and Gip jumped off over the hack to the ground. He sent Gip to a friend's house and then made his escape on a cow pony, with Tom Carson and two others close in pursuit. Hardin's dun nag out-distanced the police and he reached a cow camp on the north bank of the North Cottonwood a half hour ahead of his pursuers. He armed himself with two six-shooters and a Winchester. He dropped down under the bank when the officers rode up. They asked the cook where Hardin was. He told them he had gone to the herd and invited them to get down and have some dinner. While they were eating, Wes stepped up, and covering Carson with his Winchester, said,

"All hands up, or I'll shoot."

They threw up their hands and he told the cook to take their guns from them. After they had finished their meal, Hardin forced all three to take off their boots and clothing, and sent them on their forty-mile journey home in their underwear.

In July a group of citizens petitioned the Council to reduce the police force one-half, in other words discharge two policemen. The petition was referred to a committee. On September 2, the Council passed one motion discharging McDonald and Gainsford for the reason that their services were no longer needed, and another directing the Marshal to suppress all dance houses. Evidently Wild Bill executed the order effectively. On September 14, the local paper reported that during the preceding ten or twelve days "almost every eastbound train" had "carried away a vast multitude of sinful humanity. Prostitutes, pimps, gamblers, cappers and others of like ilk finding their nefarious vocations no longer remunerative" were embracing this opportunity to go to Newton or some other city. Gainsford went to Great Bend and was employed there as a policeman.

That summer hard feelings developed between Wild Bill and the Texans headed by the proprietors of the Bull's Head. Wes Hardin states that soon after he came to Abilene he found that Ben Thompson disliked Wild Bill. Ben tried to induce Wes to kill Bill. Wes told him,

"I am not doing anybody's fighting just now except my own, but I know how to stick to a friend. If Bill needs killing, why don't you kill him yourself?"

"I would rather get someone else to do it," was Ben's answer; and he probably told the truth. When two gunmen of their caliber clashed, neither could be too sure of the outcome.

The origin of the enmity between Hickok and the Texans

is not known. Ben Thompson's friends explain it under two heads: First, Wild Bill and other city officials were permitting crooks to fleece Texans and were sharing the spoils, which state of affairs was actively opposed by the proprietors of the Bull's Head; Second, Wild Bill and Coe came to blows in the Gulf House over Jessie Hazel, a beautiful member of the Cyprian Sisterhood who showed a decided preference for Phil. They stated that Hickok did not take his defeat graciously; instead chewed his mustache and vowed that he would put his rival out of the way. The Wild Bill enthusiasts find evidence to refute these charges. They say that Coe became angry when Bill reprimanded him for cheating at cards. Furthermore, they believe that Coe planned to kill the Marshal. Their contention is supported by statements made in two contemporary newspapers. The Abilene *Chronicle* contained the following reference to the hostile feelings existing between the two men:

"It is said that he (Coe) had a spite at Wild Bill and had threatened him—which Bill believed he would do if he gave him the opportunity." The Junction City *Union* stated that Coe had threatened to put Bill out of the way "before frost."

On Thursday evening, October 5, a group of Texans, who planned to start home next morning, were on a farewell spree in Abilene. Phil Coe was going to Texas with the boys and took part in the frolic. He did not usually carry a gun, but that evening he put on a six-shooter. The reveling began about sunset. The merrymakers seized Jake Karatofsky and carried him on their shoulders to the Applejack Saloon where they forced him to treat the crowd. They compelled a number of others to stand treats. It is said that they caught some of the boys, tore their clothes off, and carrying them into a clothing store, fitted them out better and more completely than they were before. It was a rough kind of fun, but everyone seemed to be in a jolly mood. Then the revelers sought

Wild Bill who was found in a restaurant. He refused to take part in the bacchanalian festivities but invited them to drink at his expense at the bar of the Novelty Theatre, admonishing them to keep within the bounds of order or he would stop their celebration.

It was now about nine o'clock. One account says Wild Bill and Mike Williams, a policeman, remained at the Novelty Theatre, for trouble would most likely break there. According to the Thompson version, the boisterous group caught Wild Bill a hundred yards or so east of the main street, and stripping him from head to foot, carried him on their shoulders to a clothing store and fitted him out with the best suit of clothes that could be purchased. Leaving Bill at the store, they went west on First Street to Cedar when a savage dog tried to bite Phil. He pulled out the pistol and shot the dog. The revelers, numbering about fifty, then turned north and stopped at the Alamo Saloon, the three double-glass doors of which were wide open.

Hearing the shot, Wild Bill ran up the alley, either from the theatre or the clothing store, to the rear door of the saloon which he entered. Coming toward the front, he roughly inquired who had done the shooting and denounced the bad faith of the merrymakers. He was confronted by Coe, who stood with his revolver in his hand, as did the others in the crowd. In response to the Marshal's second inquiry, Phil said,

"I fired the shot; I shot at a dog."

Bill believed that this meant trouble, and quick as a flash, threw two revolvers on the Texan. The two men were not over eight feet apart and both fired almost simultaneously. Several shots were exchanged. Bill shot his antagonist in the abdomen, exclaiming,

"I've shot too low."

Coe's first shot went through Bill's coat grazing his side. He fired another which passed between the Marshal's legs and struck the floor. At this moment Mike Williams, having heard the firing, came running around the corner from the Novelty Theatre and down the dark sidewalk for the purpose of assisting Bill. The latter, surrounded by the crowd and standing in the light, did not recognize the policeman and shot him twice, killing him instantly. Two men in the crowd were hit, one of them seriously.

Wild Bill was furious. He declared an end to the festivities, ordering the cowboys from the streets, and went from street to street dispersing the crowds of angry and excited men.

Phil was taken to his cottage near the school house in the southwest part of town. Next morning the children came to school all excited. On the playground they gathered in groups, discussing the tragedy and watching them make a desperate effort to save Phil's life. Not much studying was done that day. As the pupils tried to study their lessons, their thoughts wandered repeatedly to the little home across the way where death crept slowly upon the big handsome gambler. Phil lived in great agony until Sunday evening when he died.

Coe's body was taken to Texas for burial by his friend Bud Cotton. On the road, Bud overtook Ben Thompson who was returning to Austin with his family. Ben and his wife and little boy had been injured in Kansas City that summer when a buggy in which they were riding overturned. They had recovered sufficiently so that they could travel homeward by easy stages. While Ben, with his head resting on the casket, wept like a child over the loss of his friend, Bud related the sad story of the tragedy.

Mike Williams' body was taken to Kansas City where his family were living. Wild Bill paid the funeral expenses. The afternoon of the tragedy, Williams received a telegram from his wife calling him home because she was seriously ill. He intended to go home on the 9:45 Denver express that evening. Before the train left Abilene, death had claimed him.

Immediately after the tragedy, Wild Bill made arrangements to prevent further disturbance and bloodshed. Additional policemen were put on duty. Bill procured a shotgun and cut off both barrels. He carried this, as well as his pistols, never leaving it out of his reach day or night.

The cattle season over, Hickok's services as Marshal terminated. On December 12, the City Council passed a resolution discharging him "for the reason that the city is no longer in need of his services and that the date of his discharge take place from and after the 13th day of December, A.D. 1871." Wild Bill submitted a full report of the fines collected for the period of his incumbency in office; then he left Abilene and went on the stage for a time.

The following year the Texas cattle trade shifted to other market places. The rough element and a considerable number of business men followed it. The glamorous days were over, never to return. Abilene became a quiet little "City of the Plains."

ELLSWORTH[2]

The visitor in Ellsworth today sees a modern city with a population of some two thousand law-abiding citizens, excellent schools, good churches, and other up-to-date civic improvements. As he looks upon these marks of progress and the evidences of respect for authority, he can scarcely believe that only three score years ago this place was one of the wildest towns of the West; that many men in those days were wont to settle their disputes with firearms instead of waiting for the action of a slow judicial tribunal, and as a result more than one man died with his boots on; that for a time, according to tradition, a self-appointed vigilance committee hanged those whom they wanted out of the way to the old cottonwood tree down by the river and required some of the town's folk to accompany them to make the lynching party respectable; and that "Lady Godiva of the Plains," in performing her part in a wager, walked down the main street in broad daylight, carrying a six-shooter in each hand, but because of her record as a markswoman not a man looked at her. These and many other stories make up the folk-say of the community. In fact the early history of Ellsworth is so colored by the dramatic in life that it might appropriately be called the "town of tragedies."

The town site was laid out in the spring of 1867. In June a flood caused the Smoky Hill to overflow and put Ellsworth four feet under water, washing some of the frail frame houses from their foundations. Then the inhabitants decided to move to a new site on higher ground two miles to the northwest. Scarcely was the new site surveyed when two other misfortunes were visited upon the community. The Indians committed depredations in the vicinity and cholera broke out in town and at Fort Harker. Three disasters in rapid succession were too much for these hardy pioneers; they were discouraged and began to leave. In a short time the population dwindled from about 1,000 to less than 50.

Then a second growth took place which was more permanent. In 1868 Ellsworth was incorporated as a village and in 1871 it became a third class city. In July that year the first mayor and city council were elected and a city marshal appointed. About this time the Texas cattle trade shifted to Ellsworth and more tragedies occurred.

About a thousand people resided in Ellsworth in cowtown days. The main street ran along either side of the railroad making an exceedingly wide street or two streets called North Main and South Main. The business section was approximately three blocks long. The store buildings, mostly one and two story frame structures with porches on the front, lined the outer side of each street and faced the railroad. Here and

there more pretentious structures of brick had been erected—
for example, Minnick and Hounson's drug store on South
Main; Arthur Larkin's new hotel on North Main, re-built to
take the place of the one destroyed by fire in '69; and the
courthouse and jail a block east of the hotel. Board sidewalks
were generally in use, though in the spring of '73 Arthur
Larkin constructed a stretch of sidewalk twelve feet wide
made of magnesia limestone in front of his hotel. It was said
that no other town in Kansas, not even Kansas City, had a
sidewalk equal to it. In keeping with the custom of the times
most of the business places provided benches or seats for
loafers under the wooden awnings. There were hitching posts
in front of the stores to which farmers' teams or cow ponies
were tied most of the time day and night. The streets were not
paved; the dust was deep in dry weather and the mud still
deeper when it rained. However, during the boom years of
the cattle trade the City Council provided for considerable
grading and other improvements on the streets.

The location of buildings which were the scene of stories,
or associated with the lore of the plains, (commencing at the
west end on South Main), was as follows: Drover's Cottage,
a three-story hotel equipped with 84 nicely-furnished rooms,
and operated by J. W. and Louisa Gore and M. B. George
who had followed the cattle trade from Abilene and moved a
part of the Drover's Cottage from that place to Ellsworth.
East of Douglas: Jake New's saloon; John Kelly's American
House, enlarged and refurnished that the proprietors might
better accommodate with "luxury and ease all those fatigued
with the toils and labors of the day, and especially the Texas
drovers upon their arrival at this city after a long and weary
journey"; Nick Lentz's saloon which not only dispensed
strong drinks but was equipped to supply the unclean with
hot and cold baths; the double building which housed the general store of Jerome Beebe who had branch stores at Wilson

and Brookville and sold a variety of merchandise—in fact most everything from high grade groceries and "wines and liquors for medicinal purposes" to Kirby's reapers and Moline plows; Joseph Brennan's saloon east of Beebe's; and Whitney and Kendall's furniture store a half block east of Lincoln Avenue. Whitney was a silent partner in the firm. The railroad station was almost directly in front of Beebe's store.

The newly completed courthouse and jail were located on the north side of the railroad tracks two blocks east of Douglas. Toward the west end of that block and back from the sidewalk old timers will point out to you the spot where the shack stood in which Wild Bill Hickok lived when he was in Ellsworth. The Grand Central Hotel, owned by Arthur Larkin, was on the corner of Lincoln. The building still stands and is now called the White House Hotel. If this building could speak it would tell you that many noted characters of the Old West occupied its rooms in the early days—Buffalo Bill Cody; Wild Bill Hickok; Wyatt Earp; Ben and Bill Thompson; "Rowdy Joe" Lowe of Wichita dance hall fame; big cattle men; several local policemen; and other celebrities of the plains. Close against the hotel on the east was the Ellsworth *Reporter* Office. In the next block west, and opposite the depot: Arthur Larkin's dry goods and clothing store, in which building the City Council in '73 rented a room for the police court at $15.00 a month. Beyond were: Nagle's livery stable; a gambling place; the post office; and Seitz's drug store on the corner of Douglas, advertised as the "oldest established drug store in western Kansas." George Seitz, the proprietor, was a native of Germany and was a member of Ellsworth's first city council, an office which he held for many years.

During the first seven months of '73, a total of thirteen persons were licensed to carry on the business of saloon and dramshop keepers for the year. Three of this number were proprietors of the hotels.

The stockyards were located up the railroad tracks in the west part of the city; they were constructed of unpainted lumber and covered several acres of ground. The yards had seven chutes from which 200 cars of cattle per day could be loaded. The Ellsworth *Reporter* claimed that these yards were the largest in the State in '72. Colonel R. D. Hunter, well-known among Texas cattle men, was superintendent of the stock yards.

About a half mile east of town, there was a group of tough houses known as Nauch-ville, or the bottom. Races were held out there and the rough element had a high old time with plenty of wine, women and song.

As stated, Ellsworth became one of the leading cattle markets of the West in the early seventies. In 1871 a total of about 35,000 head of cattle were shipped over the Kansas Pacific Railroad from this point, and the following year the number marketed was increased to 40,000. The drive began early in the spring of '73. In April twenty-eight herds, ranging from 2,000 to 10,000 head each, were on their way to Ellsworth. The largest herd was owned by W. S. Peryman and Company, while Allen and Bennette drove 8,000 head, and Alonzo Millett and Major Seth Mabry were on the road with 6,000 cattle. Later in the season Col. J. J. Myers started up the trail with 27,000 head of cattle. In June the press reported that there were more than 100,000 longhorns in and around Ellsworth, and it was believed that a quarter of a million head would be received and shipped that season. "The great droves cover the hills and knolls, and the valleys are dark with them for miles around."

The people of Ellsworth made every effort to direct the cattle trade to their town and to counteract the advertising of Wichita which was becoming a dangerous competitor. The correspondent of the Topeka *Commonwealth* in 1872 pointed out the advantages of Ellsworth. He said that city had the railway facilities, the largest cattle yards in the State, and the hotel accommodations for the drovers and their crews. The cattlemen would not have to wait for promised facilities to materialize. The new trail running by way of Kingman and Ellinwood to Ellsworth was spoken of with pride and the drovers were told that they would be less liable to interruptions and annoyances than over the old trail. The total distance over the new trail from the crossing of the Red River in Texas to Ellsworth was 350 miles; the distance was shortened to 315 miles in '73 and the trail was called Cox's Trail for William M. Cox, who surveyed it.

Abel H. Pierce, known throughout the cattle country as "Shanghai Pierce," to distinguish him from a cowman of smaller stature of the same name, worked in the interests of Ellsworth. He had been part owner of the Rancho Grande in eastern Texas on which more than 100,000 longhorns grazed before he came to Kansas in the '70s to trade in cattle. His big steers, called "Shanghai's sealions," were known far and wide. Shanghai enjoyed being in the saddle with the boys and was a great storyteller. Late at night in camp one could hear the men laughing at his yarns. He talked so loud that Charley Siringo, who rode in his outfit, said that his voice "could be heard nearly half a mile even when he tried to whisper."

The cattle trade brought to Ellsworth hundreds of cowboys, and the rough element which moved from town to town with the shifts of the trade, congregated here. A visitor in 1872 had this to say of the new market:

"This little border town of Ellsworth is not the most moral one in the world. During the cattle season, which, I am told, only lasts during the summer and fall, it presents a scene seldom witnessed in any other section. It reminds one of a town in California in its early days, when gambling flourished, and vice was at a premium. Here you see in the streets men from every state, and I might say from almost every nation—the

tall, long-haired Texas herder, with his heavy jingling spurs
and pairs of six-shooters; the dirty, greasy Mexicans, with un-
intelligible jargon; the gambler from all parts of the country,
looking for unsuspecting prey; the honest emigrant in search
of a homestead in the great free west; the keen stock buyers;
the wealthy Texas drovers; dead beats; "cappers"; pick-
pockets; horse thieves; a cavalry of Texas ponies; and scores of
demi-monde.

"Gambling of every description is carried on without any
attempt at privacy. I am told that there are some 75 professional gamblers in town, and every day we hear of some of
their sharp tricks. Whiskey-selling seems to be the most profitable business. But there are many honorable business men
here, who are doing a heavy business."

Late in the spring of '73 Ben Thompson arrived in Ellsworth. A few days later his brother Billy, who had been in
town the previous season, came up the trail with some cattlemen. Ben intended going into the saloon business in Ellsworth,
but finding this overdone he dealt some in live stock, and he
and Billy gambled, devoting much of their time to faro, a popular gambling game on the frontier.

Early that season Cad Pierce and Neil Cain came to Ellsworth from Austin, Texas. Cain, whose father resided about
twelve miles northeast of that city, owned a herd of longhorns which he evidently drove up the trail to market. Cad
was a handsome, well-dressed man about six feet tall, light
complexion, weight about 175 pounds—an almost perfect
specimen of physical manhood. Cain resembled Pierce in
physical appearance but his hair and eyes were dark. Both men
spent much of their time in Ellsworth gambling. John Sterling, another gambler, was also in town that season. He was an
erratic fellow who had considerable money and usually won
whether the bet was a good one or not.

The shipping season of '72 passed with only one shooting

affray. This occurred late in July at the Ellsworth Billiard Saloon. A man named Kennedy entered the room, went behind the bar, picked up a revolver, walked over to a table at which I. P. Olive was seated playing cards, and fired five shots at him. The difficulty arose over a game of cards in the afternoon, Kennedy accusing Olive of unfair dealing. The latter did not return the fire but someone shot Kennedy making a flesh wound in his hip. Olive was seriously wounded but the skill of the doctors saved his life. Kennedy was arrested and removed to South Main Street where he was put in charge of three policemen; but aided by friends he escaped through a window during the night.

Business was brisk during the season of 1873. That summer Ellsworth was called the liveliest town on the plains; and it was one of the busiest. All the hotels were filled with guests. Beebe's store did twice as much business as in 1872 and other firms did a like volume of business.

However, good order was maintained by the authorities, and until late in the summer, it looked as if the season would pass with nothing more serious than violations of the drunk and deadly-weapon ordinances. The police force was reduced in July and again in August. When John Robinson's circus came to town August 6, extra policemen were hired but there was not a bit of disturbance all day, which led the editor of the local paper to wonder if the extra police were put on to watch the lion. Then, nine days later, the first of a series of tragedies occurred which gave Ellsworth several months of fame as the wildest cow town of the West.

Just a few words about Ellsworth officials in the summer of '73 and the measures taken by them to fend off trouble. James Miller, who had been Probate Judge, Clerk of the District Court, and salesman of the railroad lands, was Mayor, having been elected to that office in June. The City Council consisted of five substantial citizens: George Seitz, J. W. Gore, H. D.

Stebbins, Andrew Schmitt, and John Kelly; the last mentioned was elected in June to fill the vacancy created by the resignation of Nick Lentz.

Ellsworth's police protection was adequate unless a violent form of lawlessness broke out in the city. All the officers were brave and experienced men. Chauncey B. Whitney, Sheriff of Ellsworth County, familiarly known as Cap Whitney, was a Civil War veteran, one of Forsyth's scouts in the Battle of the Arickaree, receiving a commission for meritorious service, and then was first lieutenant, Company A of a State battalion called into service against the Indians in 1869. When Ellsworth County was organized, he was appointed Deputy Sheriff, and received the appointment of City Marshal of Ellsworth in July, 1871, when the second grade form of government became effective in that town, which position he held until he assumed the duties of Sheriff early in '72. He married Miss Nellie Henry, whose sister was married to John Montgomery, then editor of the Ellsworth *Reporter* and at present publisher of the Junction City *Union*, who has supplied valuable information for this story. Ed. O. Hogue, the Deputy Sheriff, was a native of France, had served as policeman of Ellsworth city in 1872; had been promoted to the office of City Marshal, which position he held for about two months. He continued on the city pay roll as policeman the following spring and summer and was serving the second year as Deputy Sheriff of the county.

At the opening of the shipping season in '73, the city police force consisted of a marshal and four deputies who were appointed by the mayor with the approval of the council. John W. (Brocky Jack) Norton, who had followed the cattle trade from Abilene in 1872, was City Marshal. He was employed early that year as a special policeman and in the fall was promoted to the office of Marshal. Early in 1873 Norton was re-appointed Marshal, and later Ed Hogue, John De-

Long, John Morco, and John S. Brauham were employed as policemen. John Morco, an illiterate fellow, commonly called Happy Jack, had come from California in the spring of '73 and claimed to have been an Indian fighter and to have killed twelve white men on the Pacific Coast. Little is known of the previous record of DeLong and Brauham beyond the fact that they were experienced gunmen. The four "Johns" on the force were referred to as Brocky Jack, Happy Jack, Long Jack, and High Low Jack. Each policeman was assigned a regular beat and rather definite duties.

Everything ran along smoothly during the early part of the summer, nothing more serious occurring than violations of the drunk and deadly-weapon ordinances. The arrests of these disturbers of the peace averaged one or more a day. Lawless Texans were brought into the police court the same as other violators of the law. Happy Jack Morco was especially active in making arrests. By midsummer the councilmen decided to reduce the force, convinced that a smaller number could maintain order. Accordingly, they discharged Brauham on July 19 and DeLong on August 12, thus reducing the regular force from five to three.

Vincent B. Osborne was Police Judge during the cow town days, and, as might be expected, most of his work in that office came during the cattle season. In two months in the summer of '73 he passed judgment in more than sixty cases in his court room over Larkin's dry goods store.

Prominent among the cases before his court were those of Billy Thompson arrested twice that summer; the first time by Ed Hogue when he paid a fine of twenty-five dollars and costs; the second time by Happy Jack on the charge that on June 30 he "did then and there unlawfully and feloniously carry on his person a deadly weapon commonly called a revolver and was unlawfully disturbing the peace and did unlawfully assault one John Morco." This case, which is number

142 in the old Police Court Docket, was tried on July 1. Five witnesses were subpoenaed; among these were Sheriff Whitney for the prosecution and Henry Inman, the noted newspaper man and writer, for the defense. Billy pleaded guilty of "carrying a six shooter and being drunk." After hearing the evidence, Judge Osborne fined him ten dollars and costs amounting to fifteen dollars—a total of twenty-five dollars; and he was "to stand committed to jail until said judgment is complied with." The fine was paid at once and Billy was released. A marshal's fee of $2.50 was paid to Happy Jack in accordance with the ruling that when someone was arrested and successfully prosecuted the policeman making the arrest received that amount.

Friday morning, August 15, presaged trouble, but not the tragedy that occurred. Another hot Kansas day was in prospect. The sun, though scarcely above the horizon, was already beating down from a cloudless sky on the dusty streets of Ellsworth and the surrounding plains. A day in one of the few groves near town would be a pleasant diversion, thought some of the Ellsworth folk. Accordingly, the Whitney family and a group of friends planned a picnic in Howard's grove, six miles east of town. With reference to this outing John Montgomery says,

"In the forenoon I met Whitney on the streets of Ellsworth. He asked me to go on a picnic with a group of friends of ours. I told him that it would be impossible for me to do so and I also remarked that Bill Thompson was on another drunk. Whitney then said that he too would stay in town for the day, since he knew that there would probably be trouble when Bill or Ben were on a drunk—there usually was. Mrs. Whitney, however, went to the picnic."

That day a group of noted gamblers were playing cards in Joe Brennan's saloon. The stakes were unusually high. Ben Thompson was present but was not playing. The evidence leads one to conclude that Billy Thompson did not sit in on the game either; but he undoubtedly witnessed it and he was drinking heavily. Neil Cain was dealing monte and Cad Pierce was betting. Cad had considerable money and wanted to bet larger stakes than Neil was willing to take. Pierce called to Ben and said,

"Send me a man who will take my over-bets on Neil's game." Ben saw John Sterling near by and knew that he bet high and usually won. Calling to Sterling, he said,

"Cad wants to bet more than Neil is willing to pull for. If you want the 'extra' you can take it." Sterling's reply was,

"Ben, I'll take him for all Neil don't want, but say, Ben, if I win, consider yourself one-half in."

Sterling had been drinking some when he started to play. As the game progressed he continued to drink until he lost control of his better senses. After he had won over a thousand dollars of Cad's money, he put it in his pocket and started off.

About three o'clock in the afternoon, Ben Thompson accosted Sterling in Nick Lentz's saloon, and in the presence of Happy Jack Morco, the policeman, asked for a settlement on the money won in the card game. This made Sterling angry, and knowing that Ben was unarmed, he struck him in the face. Thompson started for Sterling when Happy Jack stepped up and drew his six-shooter on him. Ben told Jack not to interfere but to mind his own business and take that drunken man away. Happy Jack and Sterling went out on the sidewalk and up the street west toward Jake New's saloon. Thompson went to Brennan's saloon where Cad Pierce and other Texans were loitering. A few minutes later, Ben was in conversation with Cad in the back part of the saloon; Sterling and Happy Jack came to the front door, the former armed with a shot gun and the latter with one or more pistols. One of them called out in a loud tone, "Get your guns you damned Texas sons of bitches and fight." Then they went up the street and remained somewhere between the saloon and New's corner. This challenge created considerable excitement in the saloon. Ben asked several of the Lone Star men for a pistol or arms but could not get any, whereupon he ran out of the rear door and up the back way to Jake New's saloon, seized his pistol and sixteen-shooting Winchester rifle in the back room and ran out in front intending to go out on the railroad, where bystanders would not get hit, and fight it out.

At the same time Billy also rushed to New's saloon and grabbed Ben's double-barreled breech-loading shotgun. This gun was a present from Cad Pierce and was worth about $150. The brothers met in front of the saloon. Ben says that Billy had both barrels of his gun cocked and was handling it rather carelessly. Just then one barrel went off, the charge striking the lower part of the sidewalk near the feet of Major Seth Mabry and Captain Eugene Millett who were standing in front of the saloon. Ben took the gun from Billy and started to remove the shells when someone said to him,

"Look out Ben, those fellows are after you!"

Ben handed the gun back and ran to the railroad, followed closely by Billy carrying the shot gun.

Meantime, a crowd had gathered around the door of Lentz's saloon curious to learn the cause of the trouble. John Sterling, Happy Jack Morco, and Brocky Jack Norton were in the saloon. Everyone was excited. Someone hallooed so loud that John Montgomery, who was at work in the *Reporter* office across the tracks in the next block, heard him. There was good reason for the excitement. John Sterling had slapped Ben Thompson's face and he was on the war path.

When the Thompson brothers reached the railroad near the west end of the depot they stopped and Ben shouted,

"You Texas murdering sons of bitches get your guns; if you want to fight here we are."

At this point Sheriff Whitney tried to quiet the disturbance.

He was unarmed and in his shirt sleeves at the time. Some witnesses say he was on North Main Street. Others say he came out from the crowd on the south side. It seems probable that he was standing in front of Seitz's drug store and that when the crowd gathered at the Lentz saloon he went across the track where it was. It is said that Brocky Jack Norton started outside to arrest Ben and Bill when Whitney stopped him saying,

"They will shoot you. I will go; they will not harm me." The Sheriff walked out to the Thompsons and said,

"Boys, let's not have any fuss or any difficulty."

Ben replied that they did not want any trouble but would defend themselves if the other parties wanted to fight.

"Put up your guns and I will see that you are protected," Whitney promised.

"I am satisfied that you will. We will go to the saloon and take a drink and get Billy to put his gun away," said Ben.

The three went toward Brennan's saloon, the Sheriff walking between the brothers, and engaged in a friendly conversation as they crossed the street. When they reached the saloon Billy went in, followed by Whitney. Ben was in the rear and just as he stepped into the doorway W. A. Langford, a Texas farmer and cowman, who was standing in front of the saloon, called to him,

"Look out, Ben; here they come with guns!"

When this warning was given, Ben whirled around and saw Happy Jack coming on the run down the street toward Brennan's, armed with one or two six shooters. Ben started toward Beebe's store with his Winchester in readiness. The cry of warning created considerable commotion in the saloon. The Sheriff rushed out and went toward Beebe's a few steps behind Ben, stopping on the inside of the walk near the mouth of the alley between the saloon and the store, and called out,

"What does all this mean?"

When Jack got along by Beebe's, Ben brought his rifle down on him; the former yelled, "What the hell are you doing" and ran into the store. Ben fired at him, hitting the door casing, which probably saved the policeman's life.

Ben had stepped forward until he was about a foot from the east gallery post of Beebe's store, and on the opposite side of the walk and a little in advance of the Sheriff. At the moment Ben fired at Jack, Billy came to the door of the saloon, and possibly stepped out on the walk, and fired his gun, hitting Whitney who was about ten or twelve feet from him. The gun was loaded with buck shot and the charge was emptied into Whitney's right arm, shoulder, and breast. The Thompsons and their friends claimed that the gun went off accidentally; that all three men were looking in the direction of the threatened danger. The local paper and many of the Ellsworth people said that Bill pointed the gun at the Sheriff who made two attempts to get out of the way and said, "Don't shoot; it's Whitney."

As the gun went off Whitney leaned over and screamed, "Oh! I'm shot."

Then he stood up straight and the next moment seemed to give way as though he was fainting, and cried,

"Send for my wife, I have received a bad shot." At the same time, Ben yelled to Billy,

"Look Billy! My God, you shot our best friend!"

Sheriff Whitney was taken to his home two blocks north of Brennan's saloon. Everything possible was done to save his life. Two local doctors, Fox and Gregg, attended him and Dr. William Finlaw of Junction City, the post surgeon at Fort Riley, was sent for but he could not help him. His lung was pierced producing an internal hemorrhage. Blood poisoning set in and could not be checked. He lingered three days, dying Monday morning, the 18th, and was given a Masonic burial.

The County Coroner, Dr. W. M. Duck, held the inquest the forenoon of his death at which six witnesses testified.

When the disturbance began, most everyone left the street. They realized the danger; and as was the custom in frontier days when a shooting scrape began, they sought shelter and watched the progress of events from behind this protection. The reputation of Ben and Billy Thompson as gunmen was known throughout the West. The crowd in front of Nick Lentz's saloon melted away as soon as the Thompsons went into the street. At the time Ben shot at Happy Jack, John Sterling, Brocky Jack Norton and Nick Lentz were the only persons in Lentz's saloon. When Lentz saw Ben point his rifle toward his saloon he closed the place and admitted that he did not see any shooting but heard some. One old timer says that he made a hasty retreat for Bill Nagle's livery barn; another ran into the Grand Central Hotel; others took refuge behind a box car on the railroad track. A few townsmen ran for their arms and some of the Texans did likewise. It is not known how many armed Texans supported the Thompsons, but it is probable that a number of them seized their arms and prepared for resistance. When trouble broke in a Kansas cow town, Lone Star boys usually aided each other. They were that way; and those who were well filled with whiskey were not only ready but anxious to start another Civil War with the Yankees, and retrieve the "lost cause" if possible. Cad Pierce was leader of the Thompson supporters and especially loud in his sanction of their acts. Walton states that during the early part of the fracas the Texans "remained forted in the hotel except a few who did not take part on either side."

A few moments after the shooting, Ben went across the street to the Grand Central Hotel. Bill went into Brennan's saloon, out through the rear door and around to New's saloon. Here he got on a horse. The common story is that he ap-

propriated some fellows's cow pony. Mr. Montgomery says
that the horse belonged to Bill and that it was in Sam John's
livery stable back of the Grand Central. It appears that Neil
Cain went after Bill's horse and held it while Bill mounted. He
rode across the street to the Grand Central. Ben met him out
in front; Billy remained on his horse, Ben stood on the stone
pavement. They exchanged guns. The shotgun was a gift.
Ben prized it for that reason and he preferred it to the rifle
which was a cheap weapon, in case of further trouble on the
street that day. Someone handed Bill a pistol. Cad Pierce or
Neil Cain thrust a roll of bills, amounting to $100, into his
pocket, remarking, "Billy, you will need this."

Ben urged his brother to go to one of the cattle camps for a
few days and await the outcome of the sheriff's wounds. Bill
did not seem to sense the seriousness of his situation. Ben is
quoted as saying,

"For God's sake leave town or you will be murdered in
cold blood. You have shot Whitney our best friend."

Bill's reply was, "I do not give a damn; I would have shot if
it had been Jesus Christ."

According to the local paper Bill "then rode slowly out of
town cursing and inviting a fight." The court records show,
however, that when he rode away from the hotel he did not
leave town. Word soon reached Ben that Bill was still in Ellsworth and he sent Mat Good to urge him to go to one of the
cow camps. It appears that Bill took time to ride down to
Nauch-ville to see Molly Brennan, his "lady of the night" before he finally left town.

Ben re-loaded both barrels of his shotgun immediately after
Billy left and remained at the Grand Central Hotel, retaining
his arms for at least an hour. The local press stated that the
street was "full of armed men" ready to defend him. The
older residents agree that this is an exaggerated statement,
though a number of Texans were prepared for battle.

Mayor Miller was at his home in the north part of town during the shooting. He was notified of the disturbance and came down to investigate. He went immediately to Ben Thompson and asked him to give up his arms but the advice was not heeded.

Judge Miller became impatient at the delay of the police in making arrests. He told them to arrest Thompson and they refused. The Mayor remarked that he would discharge the entire force if they did not arrest the Texas gunmen. Finally, the police showed evidence of action; they began arming themselves and loading their muskets, and were just ready to "rally out and take, dead or alive, the violators of the law," so they said, when the Mayor discharged the whole force. This action left the city without a police and with no one but Deputy Sheriff Hogue to make arrests.

Then Ben Thompson bargained with Mayor Miller. He agreed to surrender on condition that the Mayor would disarm Happy Jack, John Sterling, and other opponents. Miller agreed to these terms and relieved the men of their arms. Deputy Sheriff Hogue received Ben's arms and thereupon the hostilities between the Texans and citizens ceased.

Thompson appeared before the Mayor to answer any charges that might be preferred against him. He was released that evening on the charge of shooting at Happy Jack when a bond was arranged by Captain Millett and Major Mabry. The next morning Jack declined to appear against him and the case was dismissed. The story that Ben was fined twenty-five dollars by Judge Osborne evidently originated with someone who confused this episode with Bill's arrest and fine of that amount earlier in the summer.

Within an hour after Billy Thompson left Ellsworth, a posse of armed citizens started out intent on capturing him. This led a Hays editor to say that Bill "rode off with half the town in pursuit." As the squad left, Cad Pierce offered a thousand dollars for the capture of the pursuing party. The posse went about as far as Holyrood and then returned home. An old cattleman used to say that they did not try hard to find Bill; they knew his record as a gunman. Ben's account, however, gives a more heroic recognition to their effort. He says that late that evening they were still "scouring the country in every direction."

After Ben laid down his arms, Mayor Miller called the City Council in special session to obtain their approval of his hasty action in discharging the police. All five councilmen were present. The minutes are brief and fail to show the nature and extent of the discussion. As one reads between the lines and makes use of other sources he knows that a heated battle was waged behind the closed doors of the council room.

Mr. Gore moved that the "action of the Mayor be approved." The resolution failed to pass. Then a motion was made for a consideration of the previous motion. The motion was passed, councilmen Gore, Kelly, and Schmitt voting in the affirmative, and Stebbins and Seitz in the negative.

Then the Mayor appointed John DeLong, who had been removed from the force three days before this, to the office of City Marshal. The appointment was not sustained by the Council. Thereupon, Judge Miller appointed Ed Hogue to that position which was approved and he was duly sworn in as City Marshal. Miller proceeded to appoint Ed Crawford, John DeLong and John Morco policemen. The Council approved the appointments by a vote of three to two.

Thus the Mayor's action, which looked for a time like a complete change in the personnel of the city police, ended in the removal of Brocky Jack Norton from the office of Marshal; the promotion of Ed Hogue to first place; the continuation of Happy Jack on the force; the re-appointment of John DeLong who had been discharged only three days previous; and the addition of Ed Crawford who served less than two weeks and left a record which is regretted and condemned by Ellsworth folk to this day. Mayor Miller came down town that evening about sundown and took the Marshal's badge from Brocky Jack and put it in his pocket.

Ben Thompson pictures a finale to this day of excitement and bloodshed which might well have a place in the "believe it or not" column. Yet the story he tells may be true as it is corroborated in part by other testimony. The management of the Ellsworth Theatre was putting on a series of high class shows to a crowded house. That evening "She Stoops to Conquer" was played and Ben Thompson went to the theatre. While sitting there absorbed in the play, a friend tapped him on the shoulder and whispered that Billy was in town and was near the Grand Central Hotel. He says that he could not have been more surprised had a thunderbolt out of a clear sky struck him. He waited a few minutes so as not to attract attention and then left the theatre and met his brother at the above-mentioned place. In Ben's own words:

"Wm. Thompson told me that after leaving town, on the day of the shooting he went out in the prairie and layed down and went to sleep; that he was drunk and that he slept until about 9 o'clock at night. He did not know where he was; that he got up and wandered around an hour or so until he saw the lights of the houses at Ellsworth, when he came on back to Ellsworth about 11 o'clock in the night. When he came in he had no money with him and had lost his pistol. He sent over to the Theatre after me, he being near the Grand Central Hotel. I went over and he seemed to be feeling very badly from the effects of the whiskey he had been drinking and from the effects of what had occurred. I then told him that I did not think Whitney was badly hurt; that as soon as I could see Whitney, I was satisfied it would be all right; that if he stayed in town it would probably cause further trouble; and that I would advise him to go out and stay with some of the cattle

camps for a few days. And thereupon he left in company
with a young fellow by the name of Jack who worked for
Frank McGee. I heard from him every day for four or five
days afterwards but never saw him again until I met him in
Texas. He came to Texas on horseback down the cattle trail, in
company with Texans who were returning home."

The murder of Whitney shocked and then aroused the entire community. Bad feeling had been engendered and the
bitterness was intensified in the next few days. The alignment
was citizens versus Texans and open war seemed imminent.

Some of the citizens formed a vigilance organization for the
purpose of ridding Ellsworth of undesirable Texans. The vigilantes adopted a system of warnings to leave town called
"white affidavits." These were served on the Lone Star men
by some member of the clan or by a policeman. Ben Thompson learned about the formation of the committee and left
town and went to Kansas City. Before departing he advised
Cad Pierce of the secret organization but the latter had special
reasons for staying over a couple of days.

Shortly after Ben's warning, word reached Cad Pierce, Neil
Cain and John Good that white affidavits had been issued
for them. They decided to investigate the report. About 4
o'clock, Wednesday afternoon, August 20, according to the
report of the police, the three Texans found City Marshal
Hogue in front of Beebe's store. Several men were standing
and lounging about; among them Ed Crawford, the newly appointed policeman. Judge Walton says that several of the men,
including Crawford, were vigilantes. As the three Texans
came up Cad called out in a loud voice:

"Hello, Hogue, I understand you have a white affidavit for
me, is that so?"

Hogue replied that this was not true and that Cad should
know better. Then Pierce requested the Marshal to go with
him as he wanted "to give Happy Jack a talking to." Hogue

refused to do so, giving as his reason that there had been too much talk already.

At this point Ed Crawford, who had stepped close up behind Hogue while he was speaking, now moved forward and to the left of the City Marshal and took up the conversation, saying:

"Yes, a damn sight too much talk . . . bad talk on your side. What did you say yesterday when you had that shotgun in your hands? You said this gun had killed one short horn son of a bitch, and that it cost $100 and you would not take $200 better for it."

Cad made a reply which was not understood.

"What is that you say? If you want a fight here is the place for it—as good as any!" was Crawford's rejoinder.

Then the officer stepped back, laid his hand on his six shooter but did not draw until Cad Pierce "put his hand behind his back." Crawford drew his revolver and shot Pierce in the side. The latter ran into Beebe's store. Crawford followed, shooting him in the arm, and then beat him over the head with his six shooter. Pierce lived but a few minutes. His body was sent to his home in Austin, Texas, for burial.

The gun used by Crawford either bounded into or was dropped into a cracker barrel where it was found later by D. H. Fraker who began his business career as a clerk for the Beebe firm. Mr. Fraker kept the gun as one of his prized treasures for over a half century when it disappeared from his home.

Neil Cain had a narrow escape that day or the following. The Ellsworth *Reporter* says that Happy Jack pointed two revolvers at him. Cain begged for mercy and on the intervention of the City Marshal was spared. Thereupon, he mounted his horse and fled.

The shooting of Pierce occasioned great excitement which was intensified by the fact that it followed so closely after the

Whitney murder. Then the manner in which he was killed shocked the community. Cad Pierce was a gambler, but he "minded his own business," says an old timer, and was well liked. Some evidence conflicts with the account reported to the press by the police. One source states that Pierce was unarmed at the time. Another that there was no argument leading to the shooting; that it was a cold-blooded murder. Old timers speak of the incident with regret.

Be that as it may, the shooting aroused the Texans to immediate action. A squad of gunmen rode into Ellsworth and after remaining about twenty minutes left town declaring their intention of burning it.

This threat caused the Ellsworth folk to adopt protective measures. The local press under the title of "Law and Order" said that honorable drovers were still welcome to the advantages of the city and county but declared that they must not countenance and uphold men who were liable to shoot down women and children "accidentally" in the street. The citizens armed themselves and offered their services to the Mayor. The evening Pierce was killed, a meeting was held at which a resolution was passed that "gambling shall be suppressed" and the determination was written on every face that law and order should prevail. A nightly detail of twenty reliable citizens patrolled the streets to see that no conflagration was kindled, and to suppress any disorder. The citizens' organization made a search for arms and a "dozen or so hard cases were ordered to leave." They are said to have made a raid on the Grand Central Hotel and seized the guns and pistols belonging to the Texans which had been checked there. Then the Lone Star men telegraphed to Ben Thompson in Kansas City to buy thirty or forty outfits and bring them out. The telegram was divulged. Thursday morning the wires fairly sang as this message was flashed to the officers at Salina:

"Arrest Ben Thompson who is on the train from the East."

The vigilantes, however, were outwitted. When the train arrived at Salina Ben was not on it, nor on any of them; they were all searched for several days. He stayed in Kansas City a few days and then went by way of St. Louis and New Orleans to Austin, Texas.

The Governor heard about the trouble and telegraphed Mayor Miller to preserve order and call on the State Government for aid if he could not maintain peace. Attorney General Williams came out to Ellsworth to look the situation over.

The neighboring town papers could not refrain from making wise cracks at Ellsworth's misfortune. One of them said, "The great cry at Ellsworth had resulted in a small amount of wool." The early residents do not remember much cause for concern, though the danger doubtless looked far more real then than now. Ernest Cunningham recalls that one night he was on the beat with Charlie Brown from the American Hotel to the south end of the bridge. Nothing happened to interrupt the montony of the night's vigil, excepting one humorous incident. They heard footsteps and could distinguish the dim outline of a man coming toward them. Mr. Cunningham shouted, "Halt!"

Instead of being obeyed, this command was greeted with, "Wha' di' yo all say?"

Brown was on the verge of firing when Cunningham restrained him, at that moment recognizing the figure as being a harmless darky named Saul Brown.

In view of the citizen activity, the rough element prepared to leave Ellsworth at once. A writer in the Topeka *Commonwealth* says "that class of persons commenced looking after their carpet bags, and the next train east on the K. P. was freighted with more infamy than is usually transported in one day. The 21st of August will be remembered in Ellsworth for the exodus of the roughs and gamblers." The *Saline County Journal*, on August 28, contained this brief reference to Ellsworth affairs: "Several 'exiled' Texans banished by the edicts of Ellsworth vigilantes have been in town for several days."

The popular dissatisfaction with the peace officers evidently caused the obstinate councilmen to modify their views and at least four of the five appear to have become convinced that a thorough house cleaning was necessary. On August 27 the Council met pursuant to a call from Mayor Miller. This was the first meeting since the 19th—the day before Cad Pierce was killed. All the councilmen, excepting John Kelly, were present; the Mayor was in the chair. The following section concerning the police is taken from the minutes:

"The matter of discharging the entire police force and appointing a new one was discussed at some length, which, on the recommendation of the Mayor, the Council concurring, was done. And Rd. (Richard) Freebourn appointed Marshal and granted the authority and power to select two policemen to serve under him as such Marshal."

Marshal Freebourn selected J. C. (Charlie) Brown and John DeLong as his assistants. Charlie Brown, the farmer boy from Illinois who had learned somewhere how to handle a gun, now began his long service as guardian of the peace in Ellsworth. He was well liked and in the fall was appointed Marshal to succeed Freebourn, a position he held for two years when his resignation was accepted by the Council with words of commendation and regret.

On September 4 Happy Jack was killed by Policeman Brown. He had been discharged with the balance of the police on August 27 and the following day he left town hastily, taking the evening train east. When the train stopped at the depot in Salina, the police boarded it and arrested him upon a telegram from Ellsworth charging that he had carried off a pair of pistols belonging to John Good, said to have cost $100. At the request of Mayor Miller, Charlie Brown went to Salina to give his testimony. Good also went but hurried back to Ellsworth.

Jack claimed that the pistols belonged to him and that when he was discharged from the police force he was asked to give up his arms in order to comply with the city ordinance. This he refused to do as his life was in danger because of his activities against wayward Texans. Furthermore, he evidently gave the impression that he had been discharged through the influence of the element which was favorable to the Texans when the latter threatened to withdraw their herds from Ellsworth if this was not done. He found a sympathetic audience among Salina folk who released him after a day's confinement in jail, and when "several parties came from Ellsworth by carriage and demanded that he should be turned over to them unarmed," the officers refused to do so "suspecting some intended foul play."

Policeman Brown advised Jack not to return to Ellsworth. Friends at Salina and Brookville offered similar advice. Disregarding their warning, he returned, arriving during the night on the freight train. The next day he was on the street armed but caused no trouble. He refused, with an oath, to surrender his arms and threatened to "make way" with someone before morning. Between twilight and dark that evening Policeman Brown approached him and told him that he must give up his revolver. As he still refused to comply with the request and drew his six shooter, Brown fired at him, the first ball passing through his heart and as he was falling a second shot went through his head.

An interesting sidelight on Happy Jack's career is the fact that his wife from whom he had been separated and had not met for several years came to Ellsworth that summer with a theatrical troupe from Wichita and was in town three days before he recognized her. She detracted from his fame by tell-

ing that it was four white men he had killed, not twelve, and
these were four good citizens who had come to her relief
when he was drunk and abusing her. At that time his left arm
was broken, leaving a permanent defect.

The last of the series of deaths occurred when Ed Crawford
was killed in November. After Crawford shot Cad Pierce he
left Ellsworth and was warned that his life was in danger if he
returned. Ignoring this warning, he returned on a Sunday
evening early in November. The following Friday he drank
heavily, and in the evening, accompanied by Charles Seward
and J. W. Noel, he went down to Nauch-ville. He went to
Benson's restaurant and saloon and had a drink. From there
he went to Lizzy Palmer's house. A large number of men,
mostly Texans, were in the front room. After he had been in
the room a few minutes he stepped into the hall where some
hot words passed between him and a man in one of the rooms.
A half dozen shots were fired. One ball passed through his
head, another into his body. No one knew who fired the fatal
shots, but it was believed that Cad Pierce's brother-in-law,
named Putman, did the shooting and that he did it to avenge
Cad's death.

On Sunday night, May 31, 1874, at an hour close on Monday, Ed Hogue came near being the cause of one or more
murders. The liquor that he had been drinking all day finally
made him crazy to shoot somebody and he came near doing it
at one of the saloons. After playing a game of cards and taking a drink, he stepped to the door and called upon the Texans
who were present to come to him or he would shoot them,
using insulting language. Being unarmed the men had to obey.
City Marshal Brown, being informed of the declaration of
war, hurried to the spot, and after a fruitless attempt of one of
the prominent businessmen to pacify Hogue, Brown, at the
risk of his life, disarmed him. Policeman Bessie and Deputy
Sheriff Stevens took the prisoner to jail. After a day's confine-

ment Hogue, on the promise to leave the city and keep peace, was allowed to depart unmolested.

A year or two later Ed Hogue was in Dodge City. In the summer of '76 he went to the Black Hills. One report states that he was killed out in the West.

A week after the shooting of Sheriff Whitney, Governor Osborn issued a proclamation describing Billy Thompson and offering a reward of $500 for his arrest and conviction. In December information for murder in the first degree was acknowledged, filed and entered in the Journal of the District Court at Ellsworth and a copy of the information was sent to the Governor. The following spring a copy of the information was furnished the county attorney to send to Texas.

Thompson was a fugitive from justice for over three years. His movements during that time are not known and are outside the province of this story. Suffice to say that for several weeks during the fall of '76 he was staying at the home of Neil Cain and probably would not have been caught had he not been with questionable companions.

Late in October a herd of cattle, eighty-five of which had been stolen in the counties of Llano, Mason, Gillespie, and Blanco west of Austin, was being driven in the direction of Rockdale for shipment. Eb Stewart, Neil Cain, Frank Enox, and several others were in charge of the drove. Somewhere near Austin the herd was separated; a small portion, which had been regularly inspected in Llano, passed near the city while the larger herd of stolen cattle was driven around the city.

A warrant for the arrest of Stewart was placed in the hands of Captain J. C. Sparks of Company C, Frontier Battalion of Rangers. He left Llano with nine rangers on the 25th and followed the herd, arriving at Austin the next day. Here Sheriff Corwin of Travis county informed him that a small herd of cattle was grazing about thirteen miles northeast of town. He immediately started with his men for the point indicated and found the two herds, discovering them about sunset just as the stolen cattle were being penned for the night at "Old Man Cain's" about twelve miles northeast of Austin. When the rangers rushed upon them, Stewart and others attempted to escape. A few shots were fired at Stewart and he surrendered. They caught sight of Neil Cain but he escaped. Billy Thompson was sitting on the corral fence watching the men pen the cattle when the rangers dashed up. He was unarmed and made no resistance or attempt to escape as he had no connection with cattle rustling and did not believe that he was one of the parties wanted. Hoping to collect the rewards offered for him for the killing of a soldier in a house of ill-repute in Austin some ten years prior to this and for the killing of Sheriff Whitney, Captain Sparks arrested Billy and brought him and Eb Stewart to Austin and lodged them in jail about one o'clock that night.

Frank Enox and George Gladdon, another notorious character reported with the gang, were not found.

The next morning there began an almost endless battle of law and wits to keep Thompson under arrest, which makes the historian chuckle today and must have seemed at least half humorous at that time to the principal actors in the drama. Ben was on hand to render assistance. He employed and paid the attorneys and used all his influence to get Billy from Captain Sparks and prevent his being taken to Kansas. Billy was taken out under a writ of habeas corpus and brought before Judge Smith of the County Court. After a brief examination the Judge discharged the prisoner on the ground that no complaint had been lodged against him. Then Billy was arrested by Captain Sparks on a warrant just sworn out in Travis County charging him with cattle stealing and again was placed in jail. The same day he was brought before Justice Tegener to answer this charge and after a hearing was discharged.

That morning Captain Sparks had telegraphed to Sheriff

The Hide Hunter

From Root and Connelley's "The Overland Stage to California"

Stage Station at Fort Kearney, 1863

Pilgrims on the Plains

Sketch by Theo. R. Davis, "Harper's Weekly," 1869

From the Rose Collection

John Custer's Old Chuck Wagon

Approaching Dust Storm

Ben Thompson, 1872

Billy Thompson, 1872

From the Rose Collection

From the Rose Collection

"Bear River" Tom Smith,
First Marshal of Abilene, Kansas

A. B. Webster,
Mayor of Dodge City

"Bat" Masterson

Ellsworth, Kansas, 1872

Dodge City, 1878

Bird's-Eye View of Dodge City, 1888

Cowboy Band on the Round-up, Indian Territory

From the Rose Collection

Forty Thousand Buffalo Hides, Dodge City, 1877

From the Rose Collection

A Herd of Texas Cattle, Dodge City, 1878

Chauncey B. Whitney
Sheriff of Ellsworth County, Kansas

Col. Brick Bond

Chuck Wagon on Round-up

Photo by H. M. Steele

"Harper's Weekly," 1871

Buffalo Bulls Protecting a Herd from Wolves

"Harper's Weekly," 1877

A Day's Still Hunting

Samuel Hamilton of Ellsworth County inquiring if a warrant was still in force for Billy for the murder of Whitney. Sheriff Hamilton wired that there was a warrant and that a requisition would be sent if desired. Sparks telegraphed back to send the requisition at once.

Billy left Judge Tegener's court believing that his troubles were over, but just as he reached the bottom of the steps he was re-arrested by Captain Sparks on a warrant issued by Judge Turner of the District Court charging him with the murder of Sheriff Whitney. The Captain started the prisoner to jail in the custody of four men but when they arrived at the jail the Sheriff declined to receive the prisoner. Hesitating to conflict with Corwin's authority, the men let Bill go. The latter made rapid steps over the hill east from the jail. At that moment Captain Sparks, in company of Sergeant Leverett, reached the jail and started on horseback in pursuit of Thompson and arrested him just as he was in the act of mounting a horse which had been supplied by James Burdett of Austin. Then he was taken to the Adjutant General's office and kept under guard there while the Captain interviewed the Governor. After this Sparks swore out a warrant and returned Billy to jail. On Tuesday Thompson was taken before the District Court on a bench warrant, but before the court was ready to begin an investigation a capias was served upon him from Arkansas County charging him with murder and he was led back to jail. Ben had this paper served for the purpose of preventing Captain Sparks from taking his brother to Kansas.

On November 3, Governor Coke issued a warrant commanding the execution of the requisition from Kansas. Upon the presentation of this warrant Sheriff Corwin refused to deliver Thompson on the ground that he had been held by virtue of the warrant from Arkansas County. Then Corwin consulted Attorney General Boone and a process was served which detained Billy in Austin until the question of priority of custody was decided by the District Court. On the 15th the judgment was rendered that the requisition from Kansas should have precedence, whereupon Thompson's attorneys took an appeal from this decision to the Court of Appeals. Ignoring this legal action, Captain Sparks, the following morning, detailed Sergeant Robinson and two men to bring the prisoner out of the jail. They found the sheriff and jailer both absent and no one seemed to know where the keys were. David Ligon, a member of Company C who had been on guard duty at the jail, Mrs. Corwin, and an old gentleman, being found at the jailer's residence, a peremptory demand was made for Billy. Thereupon, Ligon found the keys and delivered the prisoner to Sergeant Robinson. Billy was placed astride a mule and taken to the International Railroad depot two and a half miles from Austin, and was started on his way to Ellsworth.

Captain Sparks' troubles were not over yet. Ben had not played his last card. He telegraphed to several points to have Sparks stopped by suing out a writ of habeas corpus so that he might get an order from the Court of Appeals holding his brother in Texas to await the result of the appeal. On the way Sparks feared a rescue and applied for and obtained additional guard at Dallas from Sheriff Moon of that county. The Dallas *Commerical* contained the following account of the incident:

"Captain Sparks, of the Texas State Police, arrived in Dallas Saturday morning, having in custody one William Thompson, otherwise styled 'Billy.' Captain Sparks started with his man on Friday. Between here and Corsicana, however, the officer became convinced, from the manner of a number of men who boarded the train, that a rescue was planned, to be executed about Denison, and he stopped here for the purpose of getting a guard and to provide himself with the means of defeating the premeditated rescue. His fears were confirmed by an attempt made here to get him (Sparks) arrested on a charge of kidnapping. Justice Peak, to whom the application was made, refused to issue a writ, and some unnecessary excitement has ensued. Billy Thompson is said to be a gambling desperado, who has many friends and intimates in Texas and Kansas. He has a great objection to going back to Kansas, because there are pending against him several indictments among them one for the murdering of Sheriff Whitney, of Ellsworth County. Sheriff Moon detailed a force of deputies, in addition to the regular jail guards, and also detachments of the city police and Lamar Rifles, to be prepared to frustrate any attempt to rescue that might be made by his friends, a host of whom are known to have concentrated here. Captain Sparks telegraphed our State authorities at Austin for instructions to Sheriff Moon to provide him a sufficient force to see him safely through the Indian Territory."

Sheriff Hamilton met Captain Sparks and the rangers who were bringing Billy Thompson, at Salina. The train arrived in Ellsworth about ten o'clock that night and when it stopped five men got off; first the three rangers, heavily armed with guns and revolvers and cartridge belts; next Billy; and then the Sheriff bringing up the rear. A large crowd was at the railroad station. As the party started toward the county jail someone in the crowd called out,

"Get a rope, boys!"

A second look at the three stalwart Texans and the sturdy figure of the Sheriff, all heavily armed, and the request was not complied with.

Threats of a rescue were also made and one morning a few days later Ellsworth folk were told that Billy had been taken to Salina and lodged in jail for safe keeping. "There too," says the Leavenworth *Times*, "his friends followed him and the matter became so serious that a strong guard had to be kept around the jail night and day, not only to prevent a rescue but to save the prisoner from the dire vengeance of lynch law which was also mentioned in a manner not be be mistaken. Finding it no longer safe to keep him at Salina the Sheriffs of the two counties brought him here, as stated, and lodged him in the Penitentiary for safe keeping until the time of his trial —March—arrives. He is described as a powerful man and a willing slave to the worst passions. His guards while conveying him to prison, not only had him heavily ironed, but kept him constantly covered with well-loaded double barreled shotguns. His capture and safe keeping has cost a trifle over $900, including the reward. He is now in a place where he will not be likely to receive anything in the shape of successful assistance and will await the time when he will face the positive evidence which it is thought will be sure to return him to his present quarters."

The Thompsons were in straightened financial circumstances the winter after Bill was arrested. Ben had spent considerable money in his efforts to free his brother. Bill had been a fugitive from justice for over three years and was without funds the months he was confined in the Leavenworth jail. After Bill was returned to Kansas, Ben wrote as follows:

"I always told you Billy, that you would have no show if you were arrested on this charge and I was caught broke. We will do what we can for you and see that you have able counsel. But it is a hard case and will take a good deal of money to get you out. Keep up good spirit. I will leave no stone unturned to get you clear."

Billy's trial was set for the March term of court, 1877. On the 18th of that month A. H. Case of Topeka and Phil Pendleton of Ellsworth, who had been county attorney when the crime was committed, were employed to defend him. The witnesses were scattered from Texas to Dakota and there was not sufficient time to get the evidence and prepare the case for trial. Accordingly, Bill's lawyers asked for a continuance of the case. The trial was postponed until September and Bill was returned to Leavenworth for sake keeping.

The trial began on September 5 and ended the 14th. Robert Gill, a brother-in-law, was in Ellsworth several weeks in the interests of the defense. The town paper spoke of Gill as "a fine man" who "made many friends here." The State was represented by County Attorney Ira E. Lloyd and Attorney General Willard Davis, while Messrs. A. H. Case, Phil Pendleton, and J. D. Mohler of Salina were attorneys for the defendant. The jury was selected with great care out of forty-eight sworn for the case. They represented some of the best citizens of the county and were acceptable to both parties.

Thompson's attorneys built up their defense on the ground that the shooting was accidental and presented a convincing argument to the jury. On this point the local paper said, "Messrs. Case and Mohler, two of the defendant's attorneys, are very able men and they used all their eloquence and ingenuity to save their client. The prisoner's good conduct and the sympathy bestowed upon him by some of our town's people may also have helped him some."

During the trial the jurors were kept under constant surveillance so that no undue influence might be used over them which led the press to remark: "The jurors on the Thompson case will earn their county scrip."

As stated above, the trial ended on the 14th. The jury deliberated about an hour before they reached a unanimous agreement. The Ellsworth *Reporter* describes the scene in the court room on their return as follows:

"When they came back with their verdict the court room was full and everyone but the prisoner seemed intensely interested to learn the result. Thompson came in with the sheriff and deputies smiling as if he was sure that his bonds were about to be loosed. The clerk commenced reading and just as we expected to hear the word 'guilty' pronounced he read 'not guilty,' when all decorum was forgotten by the friends of the prisoner who congratulated him on his escape.

". . . This was a great surprise to most of our citizens, especially to those who were living in the county at the time Thompson shot Whitney. They expected nothing less than twenty years in the penitentiary for him, as until this court met the shooting had not been called 'accidental.' This is the way most of our old town residents felt—that he got off altogether too easy—that the taking of human life was not considered a crime in Ellsworth. On the other hand, we have been informed by unprejudiced persons who attended the trial, that the verdict was such as they expected it would be after listening to all the evidence pro and con."

There was considerable talk at the time that some of the witnesses perjured themselves and that the acquittal was purchased. This much is certain. The trial was so expensive that it consumed about all Ben Thompson had and it cost the County $3,500.

The trial over, Billy Thompson and Robert Gill asked the editor of the *Reporter* to publish a card in the paper thanking the people of Ellsworth for their kindness. Both men left on the train for Texas the next morning. The following year in May we read in the Dodge City paper:

"Bill Thompson, well known on the cattle trail and in Texas and Kansas arrived in Dodge last week."

NEWTON [3]

The story of Newton as a cow town is a tale of wild nightlife, gross wickedness, and bloody gun-battles unequalled in any other cow town in Kansas. The Atchison, Topeka and Santa Fe Railroad was completed to the town site in July, 1871; stock yards were erected that summer; and the town became a rough and roaring market-place for Texas longhorns for one season. During those few noisy months, Newton acquired the reputation of being the wickedest and bloodiest town in the State. When the writer asked an early-day resident about conditions in Newton in 1871, his reply was,

"The firing of guns in and around town was so continuous that it reminded one of a Fourth of July celebration from daylight until midnight. There was shooting when I got up and when I went to bed."

The original town plan included a tract of land east of Sand Creek about a mile long and a half-mile wide. The main street ran north and south through the center of the tract. The railroad ran in a southwesterly direction through the town site, crossing Main Street near Fourth Street.

The town sprang into existence almost over night. The first building on the town site was moved there in March, 1871, and was used as a blacksmith shop. On April 17, the first stack of lumber was unloaded by W. A. Russell for S. J. Bentley, who arrived about the first of May and built the Newton House, the first hotel in town. Other business houses and homes were erected at a tremendously rapid rate. The sound of saw and hammer could be heard in all directions at all hours of the day and night, including Sundays. By August 15, about two hundred residence houses had been erected or were in the process of construction. Most of the business places were at that time in the three blocks north of the railroad crossing. The regular population was from twelve to fifteen hundred.

The buildings were hastily constructed. The depot was the only building in town that was plastered. The sidewalks on Main Street were made of wood and were ten feet wide. There were two public wells on Main Street: one at the intersection of Fifth Street; the other at the intersection of Sixth; each well contained twenty feet of sweet, cold, palatable water.

The grass on the town site was high and rank and green that

first summer. The streets were still covered with grass, and prairie dogs barked at passersby from their native kennels. The City Council passed an ordinance, two years later, (August, 1873, to be exact), prohibiting the running at large of buffaloes and other wild animals. For years there were no paved streets in Newton. After heavy rains, farm wagons would mire down to the hub while standing in front of stores on Main Street.

The inevitable saloon came. Harry Lovett opened the first saloon in town on the northwest corner of Main and Fourth. The Goldroom, probably the most widely-known place of its kind in Newton, began doing business on the west side of Main Street midway between Fifth and Sixth. Other saloons were established and bore such appellations as "The Mint," "The Side Track," "Red Front," "Alamo," "Bull's Head," "Parlor," and "Do Drop In." In August, 1871, there were twenty-seven places in town where liquor was sold, and eight gambling institutions were operating.

One corner of the town site, on the south side of the railroad track, and isolated from the main portion of the town, had been set apart for "soiled doves." This locality was dubbed by the euphoneous title of "Hide Park." The buildings consisted of five roughly-constructed houses, two of which were dancehalls. One dance house was kept by Perry Tuttle; the other, the Alamo, was kept by E. P. Krum. They were thirty yards apart, and around them were the other houses. The grass near the buildings was stubbed and yellow, and dim lanes worn by the feet of customers radiated in every direction. At all hours of the night and on Sundays might be heard the music of the orchestras and the hippity hop of the dancers. There was a bar in each which had to be patronized by the dancers upon the conclusion of each dance. Drinks cost twenty-five cents each. The bar realized two dollars from each dance. Besides the patronage of the dancers, the bar was constantly besieged by a crowd of spectators who were always on hand to witness the wicked festivities. In one corner of each hall was a gaming table, around which gamblers were always found at work. About half a dozen girls were on duty in each dance house. Some drank with their male partners and occasionally got drunk, shouted, and swore until a looker-on would have thought that Hell had surely broken loose. Men continually crossed from one house to the other, occasionally to seek a change of music but oftener a fresh partner.

The stockyards were located about a mile and a half west of town. They had been designed by and erected under the immediate supervision of Joseph G. McCoy, who had made Abilene famous as a cattle market. The area of these yards was 300 x 450 feet, and their capacity was 4,000 head, or 2,000 when the cattle were confined therein over night and loaded into the cars next morning. The yards consisted of fifteen sub-divisions, or separate compartments, six chutes, and a Fairbank's scale of a capacity of forty tons. Near the yards was a large and well-constructed cottage, in which the superintendent of the yards resided. There was a telegraph office in the house which was in direct communication with the station agent at Newton. The yards and cottage cost $10,-000 and were said to be the most complete and convenient of any in the state.

The chief business of Newton in the summer of '71 was trafficking with Texas cattle. Not less than two thousand drovers and buyers were in town and in the neighborhood that summer. Cow-punchers could be seen everywhere on the streets, in the gambling houses, saloons, and in the establishments in "Hide Park." Thousands of longhorns grazed on the prairies adjoining town. During an electric storm, it was quite a sight for one to look out from town and see thousands of cattle milling. It was also interesting to watch the cowboys prod and crowd eighteen or twenty of these beasts into one cattle car. By the middle of August, two thousand head had been shipped from Newton, and it was estimated that before the season ended the shipments would amount to 40,000.

In July Rev. R. M. Overstreet, of Emporia, was announced to preach in the Goldroom Saloon. At that time, there was neither church nor school house in town, nor was there even a religious organization. A horse race and a badger fight were scheduled to take place immediately upon the conclusion of the services in the Goldroom. They were all prevented by a heavy rain.

There was no village or city organization in 1871. Consequently, roughs, gamblers, homebreakers, murderers, and courtesans flocked here in large numbers where they were free from restraints of organized society and found their nefarious vocations especially remunerative. That class of mortals outnumbered the respectable folk five to two the first eight months of the town's history. A decent woman was not safe on the streets. Gentlemen associated with roughs, and gamblers appeared to be held in high esteem. Every device invented for gambling could be found in the gambling shops— faro banks, chuck luck, poker, old sledge, the tobacco box game, and a thousand other devices made to obtain money dishonestly. Each gambling house had a bar attached and later in the season, some of them added free lunches and concert music for the purpose of retaining the crowds that found greater attractions at the dance houses in "Hide Park." The gambling and drinking establishments were open day and night and Sunday, and the click of the "checks," the cry of the keno announcers, and the music of the saloon bands and vocalists could be heard at all hours.

The citizens had to rely on the township organization for their government. The two justices and the two constables lived there. One of the constables and the deputy sheriff served

as policemen. Mike McCluskie, whose real name was Arthur
Delaney, was night policeman in the summer of 1871, according to Henry Brunner, who was proprietor of the Santa Fe
Hotel at that time and at present is a resident of Fitzgerald,
Georgia. Some writers state that McCluskie was in the employ of the Santa Fe Railroad, but Mr. Brunner remembers
quite clearly that he was night marshal for about three months
that summer and describes him as a "fine looking, heavy-set,
self-reliant man who did not talk much."

The policemen received their pay for police services from
a fund raised by the gamblers. This was the tribute the gamblers had to pay for their gambling privileges, and the only
one. The keeper of a saloon obtained his license from the
county, for which he paid $150.

The first gun battle occurred on June 16 between two cowboys, Snyder and Welch, in front of Gregory's saloon; Welch
was killed. A few days later, a man named Irvin, about whom
nothing is known, was accidentally killed in the Parlor Saloon
by a pistol shot. About the first of August, a young man by
the name of Lee was shot and killed in one of the dance halls
in "Hide Park," accidentally it was claimed. Another man
was killed by being thrown violently from a wagon while
drunk.

On Friday, August 11, an election was held in Newton in order that the people might vote on the proposition of subscrib-
ing $200,000 in county bonds to the Wichita and Southwest-
ern Railroad. William Wilson, *alias* William Bailey, a Texas
gambler, who was reputed to have killed two or three men in
drunken brawls, served as special policeman at the polls. He
was of medium height, had dark brown hair, and wore good
clothes and boots of the highly-embellished leather then in
style. While on duty at the election, he was abusive, insulting,
and domineering.

About eight o'clock that evening, McCluskie met Bailey in

the Red Front Saloon, which was located on the east side of Main Street between Fifth and Sixth. Bailey was drunk and asked McCluskie to set up the drinks. The latter refused, whereupon the former, with an oath, assaulted him. Some blows were struck. The Texan ran across the street and stood in a stooping position in front of the Blue Front store. At that moment, McCluskie reached the sidewalk in front of the Red Front Saloon and fired two shots at Bailey. The first bullet missed him and lodged in the door of the Blue Front store. The second shot hit the gambler in the right side; the ball plowed through his body and lodged below his heart. He was carried to the Santa Fe Hotel nearby and placed on a bed upstairs. His "lady of the night," having heard of the tragedy, rushed up and followed the men upstairs, crying,

"Oh, my baby! Oh, my baby!"

Bailey died the next morning and was buried on Boot Hill. An effort was made to procure a man to offer a prayer at the grave, but the result was fruitless as no one was accustomed to the business.

McCluskie fled and no effort was made to apprehend him, for the unanimous verdict of the citizens was that the shooting was justified.

The Texans felt differently. Bailey was popular among his fellows. Good natured, generous, dangerous only when maddened by liquor, his bad qualities were overlooked. Texas sympathy was aroused. As the Lone Star men pondered over his death and discussed it among themselves, they became angry. A small group swore to avenge his death and declared "war" on McCluskie should he ever return to town. The leader of this group was Hugh Anderson, who was with one of the herds on the Newton prairies. He came from Bell County, Texas, and was a reckless young fellow, who is said to have participated in one or two gun fights in his home state.

Early in July, he had helped Wes Hardin capture Bideno, the Mexican, who had murdered Billie Chorn on the North Cottonwood. Jim Wilkerson of Kentucky, and William Garrett, Henry Kearnes, and other Lone Star men stood ready to aid Anderson. Two of these men lived in Anderson's home town in Texas. They gathered about their leader, formulated their plans, and molded the bullets with which they intended to shoot the "murderer" of their friend.

McCluskie returned to Newton and was there on Saturday night, August 19. Hearing that he had returned, Anderson came to town with his henchmen and selected Perry Tuttle's dance hall as the seat of hostilities. McCluskie was warned that his life was in peril, but thinking himself proof against powder and ball, scorned the warning and went across the tracks to the dance house.

At this time, a tall, young Texan by the name of Jim Martin was boarding at the Santa Fe Hotel. His home was at Refugio, Texas, down near the gulf coast. He was a favorite with all the boys. They called him "Good Natured Martin." The night of McCluskie's return, he ordered a big helping of eggs and a cup of strong coffee for his supper, wholly unaware of the fact that this would be his last meal. After supper, he went down to Tuttle's. Being Saturday night, there would be a big crowd at the hall and he would see many of his numerous friends.

It was past midnight. The Alamo had closed. The musicians had been discharged and business for the night was over. The lights still burned in Perry Tuttle's place, and the sound of music and dancing could be heard, the wicked festivities being still in full swing. An eye-witness says,

"The moon had sought her couch, and the stars above were nature's watchers. Away out on the prairie, from among a cluster of low roofed houses, twinkled lights and issued sounds of revelry and mirth. The town was buried in repose and naught animate was visible save an occasional pedestrian, hurrying home or the ghostly outline of a distant horseman returning to his camp.

"To the casual looker-on, the scene was bewitching; bewitching through its quietness and natural beauty; bewitching through its promise of quiet and rest. Of a sudden, however, the scene changes. Groups of men walking hastily and conversing in low, hurried tones, are seen approaching the town along the road to the place where the lights still twinkle and the sound of mirth flows on unbroken."

"There will be a fracas tonight, boys, and Mac is a dead man," said a heavily-bearded man in the first group. "Texas is on the rampage tonight in dead earnest, and before morning there will be music over yonder," pointing his thumb toward the dance hall they had just left. "We haven't more than quit in time. I would have told Mac, but they were watching me, and I didn't get a chance."

Another group of Texans crossed the railroad and paused to look back. "I shouldn't wonder but what there will be shooting at Perry's before long," remarked one. "I know it," said another; "and I," echoed others. "The boys have sworn to kill McCluskie, and they are going to do it tonight. You see, if they don't," said a bushy-haired cowman who carried two revolvers in his belt.

More groups and stragglers came along the road, most of them talking in the same vein. They knew what was on foot and nearly all were actuated by the one motive of self preservation. They did not care to risk any stray bullets, and hurried away from the pending danger.

The dance in Perry Tuttle's house was prolonged until nearly 2 o'clock, when, the crowd thinning out, the proprietor gave the signal for closing. Then the tragedy began. Mike McCluskie was seated at a gambling table in the corner. One of Hugh Anderson's men sat talking to him with the evident intention of distracting his attention in order to allow one of the group to strike the death blow. Other assistants stood back watching and waiting for their leader to enter, their eyes roving alternately from McCluskie to the door. Anderson entered, and striding across the room, confronted his victim. His weapon was in his hand, and he began his death song. His words came hot and hissing, beginning low and rising with his passion until they were shrieked out, as he said,

"You are a cowardly son of a bitch! I will blow the top of your head off."

At the same time he fired, the bullet passing through Mc-Cluskie's neck. The latter arose partially to his feet, and pointing his six-shooter straight at the breast of his adversary, pressed the trigger. The cap hanged fire, and Mac, bleeding profusely and discharging his weapon, fell to the floor. Anderson fired again at McCluskie, and reaching over, sent a ball through the back of the prostrate man. As Hugh arose, his assistants discharged their revolvers. It is not known at whom they fired.

When the shooting began, Jim Martin rushed forward and tried to effect a reconciliation between the parties.

Suddenly an avenging Nemesis appeared on the scene. Jim Riley, a friend of McCluskie, entered the hall. He was about eighteen years of age, quiet and inoffensive in deportment, and is said to have been suffering from a bad case of tuberculosis. For an instant he remained motionless, as if studying the situation. Then a sheet of flame vomited forth from his weapons. It is said that Texans, stationed outside of the hall, fired through the windows. Jim Martin was hit in the neck and staggered from the room, across the area, and fell dead at the door of the Alamo. Another and another shot followed until Anderson and three of his helpers were wounded, some seriously. The wounded Texans were as follows: Hugh Anderson, thigh and leg; Billy Garrett, arm and internal injury;

Henry Kearnes, right breast, fatal; and Jim Wilkerson of Kentucky, nose, slight wound. In the melee, two bystanders were shot. The two lookers-on were railroad men and were hit by bullets intended for others. One was a foreman on the track named Hickey. He received a flesh wound in the leg. The other was Patrick Lee, a brakeman on the freight train, who was seriously wounded through the abdomen.

Doctor Gaston Boyd was immediately summoned. By the time he arrived, Martin had been taken into the Alamo and McCluskie carried upstairs in Tuttle's dance hall. Both dance houses were turned into hospitals and the girls nursed the dying and wounded. Great pools of blood stood on the floor and the walls of both houses were sprinkled with gore.

McCluskie received three wounds, any one of which would probably have proven fatal. He died at eight o'clock Sunday morning. A telegram was transmitted to his mother in St. Louis, announcing his death. Cy Bowman, a well-known pioneer lawyer of Newton, held an inquest over the bodies of Martin and McCluskie that morning for the County Coroner, Dr. E. B. Allen of Wichita. A verdict was returned that "Martin came to his death at the hands of some person unknown, and that McCluskie came to his death at 8 o'clock A.M., this 20th day of August, by a shot from a pistol in the hands of Hugh Anderson, and that the said shooting was done feloniously and with intent to kill McCluskie." As the result of the verdict, a warrant was issued for the arrest of Hugh Anderson, who, with Garrett, Hickey, and Wilkerson, had been moved to a room in the rear end of Hoff's provision store located near the Lehman hardware store. That day or the next, a wounded Texan died. On Tuesday Patrick Lee passed away and was buried in Topeka. McCluskie and the Texans were buried on Boot Hill. McCluskie's body was taken up later by relatives and removed to Kansas City or St. Louis.

Intense excitement prevailed. Aroused over the terrible tragedy, the citizens adopted measures to prevent further bloodshed. The authorities declared their intention to suppress all dance halls in the future. Tom Carson, who had served for a time as Wild Bill Hickok's first deputy in Abilene, was employed as Marshal. Tom was a nephew of Kit Carson, the noted scout, and was a fearless gunman. On Sunday evening, some of the Texans made threats that they would kill Carson. Thereupon, a large number of citizens armed themselves for the purpose of preserving peace. The Marshal and his assistants, all heavily armed with shotguns and revolvers, patrolled the streets day and night. There was no further disturbance.

The police planned to arrest Hugh Anderson as soon as he was able to be moved. Meantime, the room where he lay was guarded by a well-armed group of his friends who were prepared and anxious for a fight. This fact may have caused Carson and his men to defer making the arrest.

Anderson's father was in town. He desired to move his son to a point outside the State, where he might have medical treatment, and with this in view, he appealed to some of the leading citizens on Sunday, who agreed to help him. Plans for the removal were made. The passengers train, at that time, arrived in Newton in the evening and went east about 4 o'clock in the morning. They arranged with the conductor to have a car left on the track with door open, and that Anderson should be placed in it at 2 or 3 o'clock Monday morning, and locked in the closet of the car. He was to remain there until he was on his way to Kansas City, and thus avoid detection by the Marshal who went through the train each morning before it left.

A litter was made. A group of citizens, accompanied by some of Colonel Anderson's friends, went to the back door of Hoff's store about 2 o'clock in the morning and removed the wounded man. In order not to arouse suspicion, they carried him north until they struck the cattle trail; then followed it down to the car. The night was dark and rainy; the grass high and wet; and the ground muddy. Their task was a difficult one as they did not dare use a light.

The train arrived in Kansas City Monday night. Anderson, faint and bleeding, got off and entered a hack at the depot, which was quickly driven away. The report of the tragedy had already reached Kansas City. When asked about it at the depot, Anderson refused to talk. His arrival at Kansas City was announced in a leading daily paper. It is evident that Newton officials were not overly anxious to prosecute him, or a requisition would have been secured for his return. He received medical treatment until he was able to travel, and then returned to Texas. He was badly crippled and died a few years later.

Another tragedy followed closely the shooting affray in Perry Tuttle's dance hall. A large number of horses had been stolen in Newton and vicinity. On Wednesday, August 23, the thief was caught at the stockyards. His captors put a wagon pole across a corner of the fence and hanged him on it. They may not have hung him higher than Haman, but the job was done effectively.

Early in 1872 James H. (Pop) Anderson and others decided to clean up the town. They formed a law and order committee at a meeting on Main Street and gave every outlaw twelve hours' time to get out of town, which order was promptly obeyed. One fellow was sick in bed at the National Hotel and had to be carried on a cot to the train.

In February, Newton was organized as a third class city, and in April the first election of city officers was held. William Brooks, a stage driver between Newton and Wichita, was appointed to the office of City Marshal. Charles Baumann, a German, whose name was written into the minutes of the City Council as Charles Bowman, was appointed Assistant Marshal.

Bill Brooks was a handsome, stout-built fellow, five feet, eight inches tall, about forty years of age, and had a large head of hair that reached to his shoulders. He had been a buffalo hunter and was called "Buffalo Bill"—one of four or five frontiersmen in Kansas on whom that sobriquet was conferred. He always carried a Winchester rifle while on duty in Newton.

Brooks left quite a record on the frontier as a gun-fighter. In June he was shot three times while attempting to arrest a couple of drunken Texas men, who were making it unpleasant on the streets for pedestrians. He had run them out of town when they turned and fired at him. He continued his pursuit for ten miles before he returned to have his wounds dressed. One shot had passed through his right breast and the other two were lodged in his limbs.

A week after this shooting occurred, Brooks tendered his resignation as Marshal of Newton. Later he went to Dodge City where he was employed on the police force, being one of the earliest peace officers of that lusty frontier town. He is reputed to have killed or wounded fifteen men the first thirty days he was on duty. One time, he was attacked by four cowboy brothers who were seeking to avenge the death of a fifth brother whom Brooks had killed. He killed all four with as many shots from his revolver. On another occasion, he had a shooting-scrape on the street with Kirk Jordan, a buffalo hunter. Jordan was carrying his big buffalo gun and would have killed the policeman had he not jumped behind one of the water barrels which were kept on the principal streets for protection from fire. The ball went through the barrel and came out on the other side, but had lost its force. Friends hid Brooks under a bed in a livery stable until night when he was taken to the Fort. Later on, he is said to have been in Butte, Montana, where he engaged in other gun battles.

Another victim of the pistol in this early period was Dan

(Cherokee Dan) Hicks, a half-breed Indian, who had a habit of getting drunk and shooting up the town, on which occasions he did not hesitate to blaze away at any peace officer who interfered with his celebration. The proprietors of the Bull's Head Saloon had put a sign board with the picture of a bull on it over their door. Cherokee Dan imbibed enough fire water to make him feel gay. He was standing on the corner of Main and Fifth. Drawing his pistol, he began shooting the sign to pieces. Charley Baumann was on duty and shouted,

"Hey, you ——; what are you doing? Stop it!"

The half-breed ignored the command, so the officer shot at him, missing him. Dan returned the shots. Then Baumann knelt and took deliberate aim at the drunken man. Dan, being the better marksman, hit the Marshal first in the right thigh, then shot his right thumb off, and would probably have killed him if Doctor Boyd had not rushed out between the two men and, throwing up his hands, yelled,

"Hold on boys! What are you trying to do?"

Dan, having considerable respect for a doctor, ceased firing. Citizens carried the officer to the National Hotel where Doctor Boyd attended him. He recovered but limped ever afterward.

One afternoon, Henry Brunner, proprietor of the Santa Fe Hotel, was sitting in the hotel kitchen, holding his little daughter on his lap and talking with his wife when Cherokee Dan entered through the back kitchen door and said,

"Mr. Henry, I came to engage board with you."

"All right, Dan. You know my terms," replied Mr. Brunner.

"What are they?"

"Cash in advance, if without baggage."

"Well, I've got no baggage. Does that mean you can't board me?"

"Yes."

"You will be sorry for that," was Dan's parting remark as he stepped out of the kitchen door.

Soon after that, the proprietor discovered a hole shot through one of the kitchen windows about the height of a person's head. As shooting occurred night and day, he did not know when or by whom the shot was fired, but had his suspicions.

On a Saturday night, the half-breed, who was on another "spree," stepped into Harry Lovett's saloon, and began shooting at the obscene pictures on the wall. Harry, not slow in handling a six-shooter, pumped five bullets into Dan's body. The wounded man was carried to his roosting-place in a two-story building up between Fifth and Sixth streets. His soul soon passed on and there was another grave on Boot Hill.

Late in October, 1872, J. R. (Jack) Johnston, who had been on the payroll as a special policeman, was appointed as City Marshal, which position he held for the next six months. He was a taller and older man than Brooks and carried a revolver instead of a rifle while on duty. He, like Brooks, wore the high top boots then in fashion and tucked his trouser legs in the boot tops.

The cattle trade had moved on, and with it had gone the roughs and courtesans. The town had settled down to a peaceful hum-drum life when, on a November morning, the quietude was broken by shooting and bloodshed that reminded folk of the good old days when bullets whistled down Main Street in broad noonday and the oiling and cleaning of firearms and target practice were favorite pastimes of leisure hours. George Halliday, Justice of the Peace in Newton and an Englishman by birth, was in the Goldroom about 8 o'clock on November 7 to get his morning dram. Pat Fitzpatrick, a "hangover" from the days of cattle trade, entered the saloon, and seeing the Judge, walked over to him and asked him to set up the drinks. The Judge refused. Thereupon, the Irishman drew his revolver and fired at him, remarking,

"I've had it in for you, anyway."

Halliday fell to the floor dead. Fitzpatrick demanded a big glass of liquor from the bartender, which he gulped down. Then he left the saloon and started south down the sidewalk.

The report of the gun rang out on the morning air and was heard up and down Main Street. Marshal Johnston was on the east side of the street below Fifth. Hearing the shot, he ran into Dave Hamill's hardware store three doors south, grabbed Dave's Winchester, and ran up the street and out to the well, laid the gun on the well frame, and prepared to halt the drunken man. Fitzpatrick came down the street slowly, reeling slightly, and singing. As he crossed the street opposite the well curb, Johnston called out,

"Halt! Stick 'em up!"

Instead of obeying, Pat laughed and reached for his gun. The Marshal fired, hitting the man in the forehead, killing him instantly.

Great excitement prevailed as a result of this tragedy. Farmers came to town armed with rifles, and uniting with the better citizens of Newton, patrolled the streets, closed the saloons, and virtually put the place under martial law. On November 8, the day following the shooting, the city added five deputies to the police force, paying each $3 per day.

There were other shooting-scrapes both before and after Fitzpatrick was killed, but the bloodiest gun fights were becoming history. There are various estimates of the number killed and buried on Boot Hill, which was situated near a rivulet on East First Street. Judge R. W. P. Muse, a pioneer resident of Newton, states that twelve died with their footgear in place, while Henry Brunner says that fourteen were put to rest on Boot Hill. Other estimates range from fourteen to fifty, depending on the accuracy and purpose of the writer.

WICHITA [4]

"Everything goes in Wichita. Leave your revolvers at police headquarters, and get a check. Carrying concealed weapons strictly forbidden." Thus read the inscription on large sign boards which were posted at the four main entrances into Wichita in 1873. And most everything did go, too, especially early in 1874, when the police were lax in the enforcement of the ordinance against carrying firearms within the city limits. at that time, Wichita was reputed to be the most uproarious town on the continent, and few frontier towns, before or since, have been noisier than it was during the cattle season in 1874.

Wichita looked much like other cow towns, only larger and noisier. The leading business street was Douglas Avenue which extended from the toll-bridge across the Arkansas River east to the Santa Fe Railroad, though it was not built up solidly all the way. North Main Street was built up for about two and a half blocks, and there were a few business houses on South Main. Most of the buildings were constructed of wood, though here and there were brick and stone structures. Wooden sidewalks were still used, and in some places, people walked in dirt paths.

The most important spot in town was the intersection of Douglas and Main. The famous Keno Hall—so called because it specialized in the popular and fascinating game of keno— was situated on the northwest corner of this intersection. Across the street east, was the New York store to which the cowboys came to get fitted out when they arrived in town after the long drive.

In the second block west of Keno Hall on Douglas were

two well-known hotels—the Douglas Avenue House erected in '73 on the southwest corner of Douglas Avenue and Water Street where the Pennsylvania now stands, and the Texas House diagonally across Douglas west of Water. It was at this hotel that E. L. Doheney, the late oil operator, washed dishes and polished shoes occasionally in trail-driving days. The corner east of the hotel was called "Horse-thief Corner." This corner was a popular place for selling horses at auction, and it is said that some of them had been stolen—the origin of the name.

The police court and jail were in the basement of the old court house at the corner of First and Main streets. A huge triangle of iron bars was hanging outside on which an alarm was sounded when a shooting scrape or other serious trouble occurred.

The stockyards were located along the Santa Fe Railroad in the southeast part of the city. They were completed in time for the shipping season of '72 and were described as the most convenient in the State. The outside dimensions were 300 x 350 feet with fifteen subdivisions, twenty-seven gates, four runways and chutes. They had a capacity of about 2,500 head of cattle, or 125 carloads. An average of ten cars an hour could be loaded. A 600 driving wing was attached to the yards; also a twelve-acre pen to hold the cattle over night.

Another interesting sight along the railroad was an immense pile of buffalo and cattle bones—tons and tons of them— which had been gathered on the plains and were to be shipped to the carbon factories. Many pioneer settlers made a living gathering these bones, for which they received fifty cents a load.

During the season of 1871, Texas cattle were driven to Wichita. The greater portion of these were kept here grazing on the unusually fine range along the Ninnescah, the Cowskin, and other streams near town in the hope that a better price might be obtained that winter. In the early spring of 1872, the Newton and Southwestern Railroad was built from Newton to Wichita, and by June, the stockyards were completed. This opened a market closer and more convenient than Abilene, Ellsworth, or Newton. Almost four thousand cars containing upwards of eighty thousand head of cattle were shipped that season. The traffic in longhorns in 1873 almost equalled that of the previous year. Wichita continued to be the leading northern market through 1874 and 1875 when a large part of the trade shifted to Dodge City.

A tough district, known as Delano, was located at the west end of the Douglas Avenue bridge. It was the center of much of the wild night-life of the community. There were two dance halls and a few shacks out there. The dance houses stood side by side. One was run by Joseph (Rowdy Joe) Lowe and his wife Kate; the other by John (Red) Beard.

Rowdy Joe was a short, heavy set man who had a rough way about him, from which characteristic he received the sobriquet "Rowdy Joe." His wife, Kate, was a small, handsome woman and had the reputation of being "straight." Jo and Kate were fastidious about their personal appearance and wore the latest style of clothing.

Joe was a frontiersman who had experienced about as much roughness as any man in the West. He engaged in a gun fight with Jim Sweet in Newton in the fall of '71, in which the latter was killed.

He had the name, throughout southern Texas, of "running the swiftest joint in Kansas." His dance house was patronized chiefly by cattle herders, though all classes visited it, the respectable mostly out of curiosity. No charge was made for dancing, but the men were expected to purchase drinks for themselves and their female partners at the conclusion of each dance. The receipts at the bar averaged more than $100 per night for months in succession. A newspaperman, writing at the time of his visit to Joe's hall, says,

"A dancing party at this place is unique, as well as interesting. The Texan with mammouth spurs on his boots, which are all exposed and a broad-brimmed sombrero on his head, is seen dancing by the side of a well-dressed, gentlemanly appearing stranger from some eastern city, both having painted and jeweled courtesans for partners. In the corners of the hall are seen gamblers playing at their favorite game of poker. Jests and conversation suitable to the place and occasion are heard."

Red Beard was well educated and had been reared in a respectable home in Illinois. What induced him to leave this environment and become the proprietor of a dance house on the frontier is not known. Perhaps it was a longing for adventure; maybe disappointment in a love affair. He was a large fellow physically, red as a salmon, slovenly in dress and personal appearance, and lazy in his walk. He never came over to the city without carrying his big double-barreled shotgun. When he went into a saloon and took a seat, he placed the gun between his knees.

On a Sunday night in September, 1872, a shooting affray took place in Delano between Charley Jennison, a resident of that place, and Jackson Davis, a young Virginian. Jennison was passing along the rear of a saloon and was met at the corner by Davis who shot him in the neck. The former drew his pistol and shot the latter through the body. Davis, in turn, shot his adversary in the right arm. Jennison turned and ran home. Davis died in a few minutes.

The first killing in the tough district in 1873 occurred on June 2 in Red Beard's dancehall. The Sixth United States Cavalry had camped south of Wichita. Some of the boys visited Red's place. A soldier and a cowboy wanted the same girl for a partner in the dance. A quarrel ensued, ending in a free-for-all fight between the cowmen and the soldiers. A stampede of girls and non-combatants took place, as they sought protection from the flying bullets. One man hid under a bass violin, his arms and legs protruding from the sides of the instrument, making it resemble a huge turtle. In the fracas, one of Red's girls was shot, one soldier killed, and two others wounded.

Shooting, stabbing, and fist fights were common that season. At least six people were killed and five were wounded in gun-fights during the year.

The outstanding gun battle of the year occurred in Rowdy Joe's dance house on Monday night, October 27. On that night, Red Beard and a party of friends were indulging in a drunken frolic in his dance hall. Then they went next door and entered Joe's place where a dance was in progress. It is said that Red's salutation to his neighbor was a shot from his pistol into the crowd, wounding Annie Franklin a dance girl who was sick at the time. The firing became general, revolvers and shotguns being used. Rowdy Joe was shot in the back of the neck with a pistol ball, but the wound was not serious. Red was wounded in the arm and hip by buckshot. William Anderson, who had been arrested earlier in the year on the charge of having killed a man in a blacksmith shop with a pistol, was shot in the head, the ball passing just back of his eyes.

Rowdy Joe gave himself up to the police and was let out on $2000 bail. No other arrests were made. Red died from the effects of his wound, a few days later. Joe was not prosecuted and continued to run his dancehall.

A marked increase in the cattle trade was expected in 1874 and the merchants prepared for heavier business. New firms were established. Jac. (Jake) Karatofsky, the young Russian Jew who had followed the cattle market from Abilene to Ellsworth, visioned Wichita as the future longhorn metropolis, and moved his stock of goods there, fitting out the most expensive and gorgeous show windows ever attempted in the city. A man named Saunders was granted a license to open a variety theatre, in which there were nightly exhibitions all summer. If the quantity of attire worn by the female performers was used as a criterion, it should have been named the scarcity theatre. At the rear of Steele and Smith's real estate office on Main Street, Professor S. Gessler, the armless wonder, put on daily performances, while nearby the child wonder and the freak pig were displayed. A hand organ ground all day long in front to attract a crowd. Across the way, a two-story platform had been erected over the sidewalk on which a brass band played from early morning until late at night for the purpose of attracting customers to the gambling booths. These, with the noise of the crowds moving about, the music of saloon bands, the vocalists, the hippity hop of the dancers, the clanking of glasses, and the cry of the keno announcers, gave Wichita the reputation of being the noisiest town between the two seas.

The rough characters flocked here as soon as the season opened. Ben Thompson was in Kansas several months that year. He stayed in Ellsworth part of the time and in Wichita part of the time. While in Wichita, he registered and lodged at the Douglas Avenue House some of the time, and lodged and boarded with a private family the remainder of his residence in the city. Ben evidently obeyed the law, for there is no evidence that he was in trouble that summer. William (Hurricane Bill) Martin and his followers were in Wichita much of the time that spring and summer. They were dubbed the "Texas gang" by the town folk. Hurricane Bill was well known on the cattle trails. In 1870, sixty head of cattle were stolen southeast of Abilene. As stated in another chapter, the drovers believed that Hurricane Bill and his men were responsible for the theft. The cattle men went to Marion for help. A posse gave chase, drove the thieves off, and recovered the cattle.

For several weeks in 1874, Bill and his men terrorized Wichita. They would ride down the streets, shooting and yelling like demons, and committing other depredations. The people lived in constant dread for their lives, and if the police did not actually grow faint when the Texas gang rode by, they did not welcome a test at arms with them. Thus, for a time, the toughs practically ran the town, defying the police and terrifying the citizens.

A few lines about Wichita's police force. Michael Meagher was City Marshal from 1871 to 1875, with the exception of 1874. His twin brother John was Assistant City Marshal in 1871, and then served a two-year term as Sheriff of the county, being succeeded by P. H. Massey early in 1874. The brothers were born in County Cavan, Ireland, and came to Kansas from Illinois. They were Civil War veterans and came to Wichita in the late sixties as stage drivers. Mike was twenty-seven years old when he became Chief of Police. He was about five feet, nine inches tall and had brown hair and blue eyes with a suggestion of a twinkle in them.

James G. Hope, a partner in the firm of Hope and Richards, wholesale dealers in wines, liquors and tobacco on North Main Street, was serving his second year as Mayor in 1874. On April 15, the City Council appointed William Smith as City Marshal. Smith had been a candidate for Sheriff in 1870, a township trustee that year, and a Councilman in 1872. Daniel Parks, who had been Assistant Marshal in 1873, was re-appointed to that position; and William Dibb and James Cairns were employed as policemen. In May, John Behrens and J. F. Hooker were added to the regular force, and special policemen were hired as the occasion demanded. The Marshal's salary was $91.65 per month; the Assistant Marshal received $75.00 per month; and policemen $60.00 each.

E. B. Jewett was Police Judge in 1874. The amount of the fines collected is probably a good index of the amount of crime. Judge Jewett turned more than $5,600 into the City Treasury during the cattle season.

At last the roughs carried their open defiance of the law too far. The night of May 25, a Texan named Ramsey and a colored hod-carrier by the name of Charley Saunders quarreled and both were arrested. Ramsey was indignant, and he and his friends planned revenge on the colored fellow. About two o'clock the afternoon of the 27th, while Saunders was attending the masons at work on the Miller building on Main Street, Ramsey walked up and shot him twice, the first shot hitting him in the ear, the second in the breast. The gang was on hand to aid Ramsey. Simultaneously with the shooting, the Texans pulled a dozen revolvers. Marshal Smith was standing near, but being threatened by the drawn weapons, was powerless. While the Lone Star men held off the police and citizens, Ramsey mounted a horse and fled down Main Street, out Douglas Avenue, and across the bridge followed by two or three hundred citizens, many of whom were carrying revolvers or other weapons in their hands. The shooting and the subsequent uproar attracted the attention of everyone in that part of town. The men grabbed the nearest weapons that they could get hold of, rushed into the street, and ran shouting after the fleeing horseman. Ramsey outdistanced his pursuers, clattered over the bridge, and rode like the wind across the prairie.

Saunders died two days later. The citizens were aroused. The day after the negro was shot, the editor of the Wichita *Eagle* warned the authorities that the ordinance against carrying firearms must be enforced. Through the columns of his paper that week, he asked the Mayor for a reorganization of the police force and a strict enforcement of the laws. Several

Texas drovers denounced the shooting and promised to do all in their power to uphold the city authorities and prevent a similar occurrence in the future.

As a result, a vigilance committee or citizens' police, consisting of upwards of a hundred men, was organized, sworn, and armed. The members of this force were enlisted from among the best and most substantial citizens of Wichita, many of whom had been officers in the Civil War, and consequently knew how and dared to use firearms.

The only evidence of a re-organization of the police force, resulting from the shooting affair, was the addition of two men to the regular force. Samuel Burris, who had done special service, was given a regular job, and Samuel Botts was employed in a full-time capacity.

Wyatt Earp, whose career as a frontier marshal has been the subject of much controversy, was added to the force as a policeman on June 17 and continued in that capacity the remainder of 1874 and in 1875. His employment so long after the black man's death would lead one to believe that he was not hired because of that tragedy.

The gang continued to defy the law and scare the citizens most to death through the month of June and into July. Late Monday afternoon, July 6, Sam Botts disarmed a Texan and was about to take him to jail when a dozen or fourteen men drew their revolvers on him. The police alarm was sounded, and in less time than it takes to tell it, forty or fifty vigilantes, armed with well-loaded shot guns and Henry rifles, rushed to the aid of the officers. Had it not been just at supper time, a far larger number would have appeared on the scene.

When the alarm sounded, S. M. Tucker was sitting in his law office talking with William P. Campbell, Judge of the District Court. Tucker kept a shotgun and a rifle in his office ready for action. He grabbed the shotgun and ran out into the street followed by Campbell carrying the rifle.

The Texans went west on Douglas Avenue and stopped on Horse-thief Corner, some of them going into the Texas House. Meantime, the citizens collected on the south side of Douglas. Weapons were drawn and ready for action. This array of men and guns looked like two armies facing each other.

Bill Smith tried to persuade the citizens to disperse, telling them that if any arrests were made some of the townsmen would be killed. Tucker came up about this time, and over-hearing the Marshal's remarks, said,

"This is the third time I've been out on this kind of a call, and we have never made an arrest. I don't care for trouble; I am used to it. Point out the man you want arrested, and I'll arrest him, kill or get killed."

"All right, arrest Hurricane Bill," replied Smith.

A complete silence came over the opposing groups. As Tucker cocked one barrel of his gun, the sound could be heard distinctly by everyone. He stepped into the street, and leveling his gun at Hurricane Bill, said quietly,

"William, I want you; you are under arrest."

The Texan started to raise his revolvers. The lawyer shouted,

"Lay down those guns."

"You can have me," was Bill's reply, as he dropped his two revolvers; one cocked, the other of the self-action type. He remarked later that the barrels of the shotgun leveled at him looked as big as stove pipes.

"Walk over to the police station," commanded Tucker.

The bad man obeyed. When the Texas men saw their leader surrender, they were perplexed, and many of them dropped their guns. For a week after this episode, searchers found revolvers in the weed patch on Horse-thief Corner. Before the Lone Star men could recover from the shock and get ready for action, the citizens lined them up and marched them over to the police station where Judge Jewett fined them $600.

Another episode—half tragedy and half comedy—occurred on the streets the latter part of the same month. Bill Smith had personally notified sixteen men, who boasted of no "visible means of bread and butter," to leave town at once. One of them, a little red-whiskered fellow named Thomas McGrath, not heeding the order, was arrested and brought before Mayor Hope. To the Mayor, he protested that he could not bear the disgrace of obeying such a mandate. Nevertheless, he was marched over to Judge Jewett's office. Unable to pay his fine, he was put to work on the streets in charge of a policeman. While the prisoner was at work, the guardian of the law threatened to put a ball and chain on him. Then McGrath started to run away, going toward the business district. The officer pursued the fleeing man, overtaking him on Main Street, and started him back in the direction of the street work.

The peace officer handled the prisoner none too gently and used words that were more forceful than elegant. The little Irishman replied in a similar style of language. As they turned the corner of Main and Second, they were engaged in a vociferous argument on the authority of the law and the rights of prisoners, and were still arguing when they reached a point on Second Street about midway between the Occidental Hotel and the *Beacon* office.

"I won't take no ball and chain," shouted McGrath at the officer.

"You will wear one, or I'll lay you out," yelled the policeman.

"You can't do it," retorted the little fellow.

"You shut up," commanded the guardian of law and order, and is said to have struck the prisoner; whereupon the latter turned on him, and a fist fight ensued. After an exchange of blows, they clinched, during which the prisoner seized one of the "Stars" six-shooters. The officer turned white and ran toward the rear of the *Beacon* office, yelling "Hold on! Hold on! Don't shoot!" Before he could reach the sidewalk, McGrath fired one shot which served to increase his speed. The Irishman pursued the representative of the law around the buildings and down the alleys of that neighborhood; the policeman managed to fire one shot from his remaining pistol, which went wild. The prisoner finally caught the officer as he reached the rear of a doctor's home and tried to wrest the revolver from him. At that moment, a citizen rushed up and separated the two men.

When McGrath seized the policeman's pistol on Second Street, the police triangle was sounded, and Officers Botts and Behrens came on the run toward the scene of conflict, arriving about the same time as the citizen. They seized the Irishman and marched him to the calaboose.

As a result of this disturbance, the Mayor closed all gambling places in the city, which were not re-opened for several days. However, the Council exempted these houses from fines during the period they were closed. The press reported that the officer's commission was in the hands of the Mayor early the next day after the fracas. However, he continued on the payroll, which is evidence that he did not resign.

The tough element had been conquered and conducted themselves in a fairly peaceable manner during the remainder of the cow town period. There was drunkenness, and probably there was disorderly conduct not reported in the press, but the roughs did not resort to open defiance of the law and engage in gun fights which resulted in death.

DODGE CITY [5]

A drunken cowboy got aboard a Santa Fe train at Newton. When the conductor asked him for the fare, the cow-
puncher handed him a handful of money.

"Where do you want to go?" asked the conductor.

"To Hell," replied the cowboy.

"Well, give me $2.50 and get off at Dodge."

Stories like this and tales of wild night life and gun battles
gave Dodge City the reputation of being the toughest town in
America. It gained such wide fame as a wicked town that it
has become the practice of magazine writers to make this
place the setting for many of their gun stories. While the per-
petuation of this impression does Dodge City an injustice, a
combination of circumstances made conditions worse there
than in some of the other cow towns.

Dodge City was located in the heart of the buffalo country.
Scores of hunters flocked here each season. During the fall
and winter of 1872, the town, then containing some five hundred inhabitants, was supported almost entirely by the trade
in skins and meat.

When the westbound train with Eddie Foy, the noted
comedian, and Jim Thompson, his stage partner, aboard,
rolled into Dodge City in the late spring of 1878, it passed an
enormous pile of bones. Thompson wondered if this meant
that they were killing people in Dodge faster than they could
bury them. He soon learned that these were the bones of
buffalo and cattle awaiting shipment to the carbon factories.
In fact, the collecting and shipping of bones was as extensive
an industry as the caring for hides. Great stacks of bones—
hundreds of tons of them—were piled along the railroad ready
to be loaded on the cars.

The slaughter of the buffalo was so terrific that the source of supply for the traffic in hides and meat began to fail. Just when the herds of buffalo were nearly exterminated, the market for Texas cattle shifted to Dodge City. The first important drive was made in 1875. It is estimated that nearly a quarter of a million head of longhorns had been driven to the new market by the close of the shipping season of 1876. The following year, more than 300,000 head arrived at the new shipping point, and the number increased each year until the annual drive almost reached the half-million mark.

During those years, Dodge City enjoyed the reputation, among Texas men, of being the fastest cow town in the country. Every cowboy wanted to see this tough place, about which so many tales of night life and gun battles were told. Dodge City was known as the Cowboy Capital, a name which was retained for many years and is heard occasionally today.

During the worst days, the south side of the railroad tracks was given over to saloons and gambling houses, while the north side was usually kept respectable. The old calaboose was a well fifteen feet deep. Sometimes four or five drunken men were put into this cooler at once and given time to become sober.

Dodge City secured some of her most noted pioneer citizens from Hays. One of the first was James H. Kelley who opened and ran the Opera House saloon and was Mayor of the city. In Hays he was known as "Hound" Kelley; in Dodge as "Dog" Kelley; while some folk, who wanted to give him full credit for his appellations, called him "Hound Dog" Kelley. Then came A. B. Webster and R. W. Evans, both with stocks of merchandise; Mose Waters, a prosperous liquor dealer; and W. N. Morphy, one of the founders of the *Ford County Globe*. Larry E. Deger, an early-day City Marshal, was also a Haysite. He was the big man of Dodge, weighing 307 pounds, and was noted for his long stories. One evening he was master of ceremonies at a dance and began telling one of his protracted yarns. While busily engaged with it, some one remarked, "Oh! Larry, wipe off your chin." Larry had not heard the latest slang phrase, so pulled out his handkerchief and began to mop his chin, much to the amusement of the audience.

Boot Hill

The first man killed in Dodge City was a husky Negro by the name of Texas, who was shot and killed by a gambler named Denver. A platform had been erected, and the darky was standing in front and below in the street. During some excitement, a crowd had gathered. Several shots were fired over the heads of the crowd when Denver fired a shot at the black man, killing him. No one knew who fired the shot until the gambler, several years later, boasted that he had done the shooting. Some time after the Negro was shot, a row between a group of gamblers and some soldiers from Fort Dodge occurred in Tom Sherman's dance hall, in which fracas three or four were killed and several wounded.

Through the first winter after the railroad was completed to Dodge City, shooting-scrapes were a common occurrence, and there was a "man for breakfast" every once in a while. Some, if not all, of those killed that year were buried on Boot Hill. Other victims of the pistol and knife were buried on this hill in succeeding years. Some of those put to rest in this burial ground were kinless and friendless persons who died a natural death. Alice Chambers was the last to be buried on Boot Hill. Her burial took place on May 5, 1878.

Early in 1879, the bodies were removed from the graves on Boot Hill and were buried side by side at the lower end of Prairie Grove Cemetery, northeast of the city. The skeletons were found in a fine state of preservation, and the rude box coffins were as sound as when placed in the ground. Only a few of the bodies could be recognized as all the headboards, if there ever were any, had wasted away, and nothing but little mounds of clay marked the graves.

Half Humorous and Half Tragic

In September, 1876, a weekly paper reported that a Sergeant of the Signal Service in the United States Army had been pelted with rotten eggs by an unknown party in Dodge City, the previous week. Two weeks later, a rough and tumble street fight took place between the Police Judge and a Justice of the Peace, much to the amusement of the lookers-on. Probably the spiciest item appeared in the Hays *Sentinel* in August, 1877, to the effect that a prostitute tried to "horsewhip the editor of the Dodge City *Times* last week."

In July, 1878, the *Ford County Globe* contained the following brief item in the news column:

"Street fights too numerous to mention for the past week, police business light." A month later, this paper told about a shooting affair on the south side on a Saturday night. An intoxicated cowboy had tried to take possession of the bar in the Comique. To this, the barkeeper objected and a row ensued, in which some of the cattlemen received bruised heads. A policeman interfered and several shots were fired, but no one was injured. The paper regretted the "too ready use of pistols in all rows of such character"; and then added this bit of information: "A horsewhipping yesterday (Sunday) morning to mar the usual quiet of one of our church members." Two years later, the same newspaper said that no less than a dozen robberies "were perpetrated during the past week."

In the fall of 1879, the local paper made the following observation:

"That we are not retrograding as a lively town may be evinced by the fact that on yesterday six men were thrown in the cooler while five free and easy fights occurred at the saloon of Messrs. Beatty and Kelley."

Indians

In April, 1877, James Cahn, brother of Joseph Cahn, a well-known clothing merchant of Kansas City, visited Dodge City for the first time, and before he had been in town two hours he had talked every man he met into a whisper on the subject "Indians." Sam Snyder and Ike Rothenburg, two jovial fellows, decided to have some fun with the visitor. They chaperoned young Cahn around the city. After he had met the majority of the people, an antelope hunt was proposed. The young man eagerly accepted the invitation and soon he, Samuel, Ike, and Mayor Kelley, mounted on excellent horses, were riding westward to the Point of Rocks, about six or seven miles up the Arkansas.

Just as they reached the hunting grounds, a band of about thirty Indians dashed around the Point and charged upon them. They came nearer and nearer each second, uttering the most fiendish yells, shooting pistols, and brandishing knives. The hunters wheeled their horses around and made a bee line for town with the Indians whooping and yelling behind them. Six miles had to be traversed. Cahn was mounted on an excellent horse. Those who witnessed his attempt to outdistance his pursuers say that his ride was the fastest six mile heat ever made in the West.

Hundreds of Dodge City people were clustered on the surrounding hills and upon the Court House and other buildings to witness the affair for the whole thing was a farce gotten up by Sam and Ike to test the mettle of a tender foot. The Indians were thirty Dodge City men decked and bedaubed in the most approved Cheyenne styles.

Cahn was greatly surprised when he galloped hatless and

gunless into town and was greeted by round after round of cheers from the greatly amused spectators. Being of a jovial disposition, he appreciated the joke, admitting that the affair was well done, and asked the boys to indulge in a lemonade, which invitation they all accepted.

Rob Roy of the Plains

"Dutch Henry is in jail" were the words that were flashed from person to person in Dodge City on New Year's day, 1879. No one asked who Dutch Henry was; everyone had heard of him, for his reputation as a master horse-thief had spread throughout the West. The owners of horse flesh were especially jubilant. This was indeed pleasant news. Hadn't they stood guard over their live stock many a night, prepared to battle Henry and his gang? Hadn't the press warned them to sleep with their horses when Henry was in the neighborhood?

The subject of their conversation was a genteel-looking fellow to have been a horse-thief. In fact, he could have passed for a professional man of German descent. He had black hair and moustache, a long face and Roman nose. His black eyes were bright and penetrating, denoting considerable intelligence.

Dutch Henry opened his career in the West in 1867 when he joined Custer's forces. Then he became a roving plainsman and acquired the reputation of being the leading horse-thief on the prairie frontier, though he claimed that he did not deserve such a reputation. When he was at the height of his activity, it is said that he was at the head of an organization of 300 horse-thieves who operated in the Great Plains region. A writer who was on the plains at that time says that the bands who stole horses in the Indian Territory would meet a band with stolen horses from Colorado at some point in No

Man's land and swap herds, the thieves from Colorado returning to that state and the other band to the Territory.

Henry's fame as a horse-thief extended far and wide. Many
tales of reckless daring were told about him; how handy he
was with a revolver; his powerful influence over his confed-
erates; how he rode his magnificent sorrel horse at the head
of his band with the dignity of a general; how quickly his
commands were obeyed; how he evaded the law; how desper-
ately he fought when pursued; and how he always escaped
his captors. His exploits were so close to the mythical that he
became the Rob Roy of the Plains. It was said that only "Six-
teen-String" Jack in his most successful days equaled Henry.

Despite the half-mythical tales, Dutch Henry did not always evade the law and escape his captors, though he was usually set free when tried by a jury. On June 15, 1874, Sheriff
Alexander Ramsey of Hays captured Henry north of Ellsworth after an exciting chase. On that day, Ramsey came to
Ellsworth armed with a warrant and a revolver. He called
Under Sheriff Stevens to his assistance and the two started
out on horseback. After they had gotten about five miles from
town, they discovered their man riding across the prairie. The
Sheriff rode after Henry and ordered him to surrender. In
reply, he raised his revolver. The officers dismounted and
fired at him. Thereupon, the man galloped his horse to Oak
Creek where he hid in the bushes. Ramsey ordered Stevens to
ride to Ellsworth for more men and guns. The Under Sheriff
soon returned, accompanied by City Marshal Brown and
Sam John. When they arrived at the creek, they found that
Henry had hidden in a cave and afterwards had crept up a
ravine. He was soon found hidden in the grass. When he failed
to answer the Sheriff's orders to surrender, that officer fired a
shot from his revolver, inflicting a wound on the man's face.
This wound and the presentation of three guns from different directions brought him to terms. He was disarmed,

brought to town, and lodged in jail. He was taken to Hays, but there is no record of his trial.

Two years later, a man named Emmerson, residing south of Dodge City, lost some horses; while searching for them, he met Dutch Henry and told him that if he saw the stock to take possession of it and return it or send him word. A few weeks later, Henry took the road to Russell, evidently knowing that he was under suspicion.

Early in the morning of June 16, Sheriff Weakly of Russell County received a dispatch from Dodge, directing him to arrest Henry. The Sheriff soon found his man, walked up to him, and presented a revolver at his head. Henry instantly clapped one hand on the hammer of the weapon, and with the other sought to draw his own gun when David Auer, a bystander, seized him and prevented him from doing so. Thereupon, the Sheriff made a lunge at Henry with his knife, but thrust it into the wrong man. A second effort proved more effectual and Dutch Henry sank to the pavement. Then he was conveyed to the Sheriff's office to await the arrival of the Sheriff from Dodge.

About eleven o'clock that night, someone fired into Henry's cell, the bullet striking within three inches of his head. Five more shots followed in quick succession, some cutting the blankets that covered him, but he was untouched.

As soon as Dutch Henry was arrested, he wrote to Emmerson, informing him that he had found his stock and directing him where to find it. The farmer found the horses at the designated place.

The accused man was returned to Dodge City and was given a preliminary hearing, but was not prosecuted.

That fall some horses were stolen in Ness County. Sheriff Bardsley of Ellis County was notified of the theft. Accompanied by his deputy, Charles Zaun, and a posse, the Sheriff went to Buffalo Station where he took up the trail of the thieves at daylight. One portion of the gang, consisting of six men, three women, and thirty-six horses, was overtaken on the south fork of the Solomon and was captured without difficulty. Leaving three men to guard the outfit, Bardsley went to the north fork of the Solomon, and crossing to the Prairie Dog, he discovered twenty horses and mules in charge of two men. These men surrendered, but three others escaped.

In the spring of 1877, Dutch Henry threatened to clean out the entire Walnut Valley in revenge for the rough treatment he had received at the hands of the settlers the previous summer. About the same time, a leader and three lieutenants were arrested at Granada on a charge of having stolen seven head of stock at Cheyenne. In July, Henry was captured near Red Cloud, Nebraska, and was held for some time by the authorities.

In December, 1878, Sheriff Masterson of Dodge City received the news that Dutch Henry was at Trinidad, Colorado, and had been for several weeks. He telegraphed the officers to arrest him which they did. Masterson went out there to claim the prisoner. He had no requisition from the Governor of Kansas, but made arrangements by which he was given custody of the man. He brought him back to Dodge on New Year's day and placed him in jail to stand trial on the charge of having stolen the horses from Emmerson in 1876.

Henry was brought into court the following day. The defense opened the trial by filing a plea that the statute of limitations had expired and the prisoner could not be punished. A jury, consisting chiefly of farmers, was called to try the plea. They brought in a verdict refusing to sustain the plea. The jury was discharged and a special venire empaneled to judge the guilt or innocence of the prisoner. The new jury was composed of city men who were not so prejudiced against a horse-thief.

The defense brought in evidence to show that the prisoner

had acted as a friend to Emmerson and had no intention of stealing the horses. Henry took the witness stand and told the story of his past life in a way to create sympathy. Then the case went to the jury; the jurors had been out but a few moments when Judge Peters received the paper on which the verdict was written. The Judge unfolded the paper and read "not guilty." Addressing Henry the Judge said,

"Mr. Henry ——, the jury have found you not guilty, you are therefore released from custody."

"I thank you, Judge, and you, too, gentlemen of the jury," said Henry and he was off like a shot. Making his way down stairs, he hastened to the back door of the court house where a fleet horse, saddled and bridled, awaited him. He mounted and rode off rapidly. His haste was due to the fear of being re-arrested. On learning there was no cause for alarm, he returned to the city where he was received with marked attention, many people seeking an introduction.

Ed. Masterson Stops a Shooting Affray

Bob Shaw was fairly bursting with indignation. He had lost $40 and was certain that Texas Dick *alias* Moore had stolen it from him. Bob ground his teeth and said to himself, "Let me get near the thief and I will drill him full of holes with my six-shooter."

When the two met in the Lone Star Dance hall that November day, 1877, he accused Dick of stealing the money, and trouble began. Someone went for Assistant City Marshal Ed. Masterson who hurried to the scene of conflict. When Masterson arrived, Shaw was standing by the bar with a huge pistol in his hand and blood in his eye ready to shoot Texas Dick. Not wishing to hurt Shaw, the Marshal ordered him to put up his gun. Shaw refused and Masterson tapped him on the head. Shaw then turned his gun on the officer and shot him, the ball striking a rib and passing around under the shoulder blade paralyzing his right arm. Masterson fell, but grasping the pistol in his left hand fired at Shaw, hitting him in the left arm and leg. During the melee, Texas Dick was shot in the right groin, making a painful wound and Frank Buskirk, a curious onlooker, standing in the doorway, received a ball in the left arm. Fortunately no one was killed.

When Professor Gunn Was Gunned

The boys of Sweet Water, Texas, in 1877, performed the experiment of giving Professor James Gunn, one type of character on the frontier, drinks of liquor, increasing the dose each day and watching the results. After a few days, he was under the influence of it to such an extent that he drew a pistol and started firing at them. Then he was driven out of Sweet Water and came to Dodge City. The first day in Dodge, he got drunk and spent the night on the sidewalk protected by the lime kiln.

A Doctor Lectured in Dodge City

In February, 1880, a gentleman who bore the name and title of Doctor Meredith came to Dodge City. He had written to some of the citizens of the place wishing to know whether Dodge would be a good field for his line of science which he designated as Phrenology and the treatment of certain diseases. He was encouraged to come and was recommended to Major James Dalton and Luke McGlue as prominent citizens who would likely take a deep interest in his cause. Immediately after his arrival, he decided to deliver a lecture that the public might understand his mission and come to him to be cured.

The old Lady Gay Dance hall was engaged for the occasion.

Notices of the meeting were printed and put up, and in the afternoon two boys were started out with bells to ring up the town. A large crowd assembled there at the appointed time. W. B. Masterson was chosen to act as chairman and introduced the speaker with a few well chosen remarks.

Dr. Meredith opened his address by saying that he had not intended to deliver a lecture, but "at the urgent solicitation of numerous prominent—"

"You lie!" shouted someone from audience.

Chairman Masterson rebuked the insult, and when order was restored, the Doctor began again. Proceeding further in a like manner, he was again interrupted by an insulting remark from someone in the audience, and by means of stern commands and threats of annihilation, the chairman brought the house to order.

Again the Doctor proceeded and was wading deep into a scientific problem when a loud and profane yell from Luke McGlue turned the house into an uproar of excitement.

At this moment, a "southside exhorter with one eye in a sling" made an effort to drag the orator from the stand, whereupon Chairman Masterson drew from beneath his coat tails a Colt's revolver and took his position in front of the Doctor. A crash was heard, the lamps went out, windows were smashed, missiles flew through the darkness, the air was filled with demoniacal yells, and shooting commenced.

After all the ammunition in the house had been expended, a lamp was lighted by which to remove the dead and wounded. But the dead and wounded had already escaped through the windows and door, and even the Doctor was nowhere to be found. Search was made and at last he was discovered coiled up under the speaker's stand with hands over his marble-like features and an ugly bullet hole through the crown of his hat.

╙╜╜╜╜╜╜╜╜╜╜╜╜╜╜╜╜╜╜╜╜╜╜╜╜╜╜╜╜╜╜╜╜

The Buffalo Range

T HE estimates of the number
of buffalo on the plains vary. All are agreed, however, that
there were several million in Kansas alone in the late sixties.
The accounts of the plainsmen, who saw and passed through
the immense herds, give an idea of the vast number of animals
roaming over the prairies. De B. Randolph Keim traveled
west over the Kansas Pacific in 1868. After he left Hays, the
buffaloes increased rapidly in number. Thirty miles west of
town the country was overrun with the beasts. The main herd
was on the north side of the track, and as far as the eye could
see, he said that the plains were black with the animals.[1]
When General W. T. Sherman and his party went from Fort
Zarah to Council Springs, sixty miles distant, in 1867, to participate in the council with the Indians, Buffalo Bill Cody accompanied them as one of the scouts. They started from
Fort Zarah at two o'clock in the morning and intended to
reach Council Springs at two that afternoon. They traveled

for hours through herds of buffalo which greatly hindered their progress. On this point Cody says,[2]

"We traveled steadily till ten o'clock in the morning, through herds of buffalo whose numbers were past counting. I remember that General Sherman estimated that the number of buffalo on the Plains at that time must have been more than eleven million. It required all the energy of the soldiers and scouts to keep a road cleared through the herds so that the ambulances might pass.

"We breakfasted during the morning stop and rested the horses. For the men there was plenty of water, which we had brought along in canteens and camp kettles. There was also a little for the animals, enough to keep them from suffering on the way.

"Two o'clock found us still making our way through the buffalo herds, but with no Council Springs in sight* . . ."

Keim, while on his trip in 1868, saw an announcement at one of the railroad stations of an excursion train which was to run from eastern Kansas on October 27 to Sheridan where a buffalo hunt was to occur. The excursion was to leave Leavenworth Tuesday morning and return on Friday, and was to stop at all the principal stations both going and returning. The excursionists were promised "ample time" for a "grand buffalo hunt on the plains," and were told that buffaloes were "so numerous along the road that they are shot from the cars nearly every day."

Colonel Henry Inman relates some incidents which will give the reader an idea of the vast size of the buffalo herds and of the ruthless slaughter to which these animals were subjected during the two decades following the Civil War. His account follows:[3]

"In 1868 the Union Pacific Railroad and its branch in Kan-

* Cody's Autobiography used by permission of Farrar and Rinehart, New York.

sas was nearly completed across the plains to the foothills of the Rocky Mountains, the western limit of the buffalo range, and that year witnessed the beginning of the wholesale and wanton slaughter of the great ruminants, which ended only with their practical extinction seventeen years afterward. . . .

"On either side of the track of the two lines of railroads running through Kansas and Nebraska, within a relatively short distance and for nearly their whole length, the most conspicuous objects in those days were the desiccated carcasses of the noble beasts that had been ruthlessly slaughtered by the thoughtless and excited passengers on their way across the continent. On the open prairie, too, miles away from the course of legitimate travel, in some places one could walk all day on the dead bodies of the buffaloes killed by the hide-hunters, without stepping off them to the ground.* "

Albert D. Richardson, the noted newspaper writer, traveled extensively in the West before and after the Civil War. In 1869 he wrote a letter to the New York *Tribune,* in which he tells about the large number of buffaloes seen along the Kansas Pacific Railroad. His letter follows.

"Along the road in summer one may ride for a hundred miles hardly ever losing sight of the buffaloes; and trains are often compelled to stop for them. The buffalo that attempts to butt a locomotive off the track may not be a prudent brute, but the locomotive that doesn't halt for him is equally rash. For my own part I am a new, and therefore zealous, convert to the doctrine of fencing railroads—against buffaloes in Kansas, against elephants in India, and against cattle everywhere. Since our experience at Laramie, I never hear the whistle for 'cattle ahead,' without a strong desire to get out and walk." [4]

In the early seventies, Dodge City was the heart of the

* Inman, The Old Santa Fe Trail, used by permission of Crane and Company, Topeka, Kansas.

buffalo range. "Brick" Bond, who is reputed to have killed more buffalo than any other hunter, recorded on the back of a blank check the number of animals which he slaughtered from November 1, 1874, to January 1, 1875. This check has been found recently in a drug store in Dodge City formerly owned by Bond and shows that he killed more than 6,000 buffalo in sixty days, an average of more than 100 a day. He employed five skinners.[5]

Between 1868 and 1881, the period in which the buffalo were indiscriminately slaughtered for their hides, Inman says that there was paid out in Kansas alone the sum of two million five hundred thousand dollars for their bones gathered on the prairies to be utilized by the various carbon works of the country. It required about one hundred carcasses to make one ton of bones; the price paid averaged eight dollars a ton. The above sum of money represented the skeletons of more than thirty-one millions of buffalo.

The hunters, the travelers, and the pioneer settlers had many thrilling experiences in their encounters with the buffalo. The stories told by them comprise an interesting part of the lore of the plains. Furthermore, some of the buffalo hunters composed songs, the words of which refer to incidents in their hunts or express sentiments common among the group. These words, usually put to a catchy tune, were sung over the range.

Buffalo Hunt With the Miamis

In 1854 Ely Moore went from Westport to the Miami Indian mission some sixty-five miles away. Here he was requested by the chief of the Miamis to attend a "friend feast" at his cabin. The next day, he was invited to attend their annual buffalo hunt. Their party consisted of 400 men and 50 squaws, 100 wagons, two yoke of oxen to each, and 200 pack ponies. They left about August 20. The first camp was Mount Oread; the next at Topeka; then they went on west in to what is now Dickinson County; from this point they bore southwest. When they were within a few miles of their permanent camp, they came up to an immense herd of buffalo which was headed in a southerly direction. It became necessary to order out a strong guard to keep the buffalo from running over them. The Indians said that this was the largest herd they had ever seen. They were forced to camp without water that night and remain there until 10 o'clock next day to let the buffalo pass.

The morning after they reached the permanent camp, a hundred of the hunters were ordered to commence killing as thousands of buffalo were feeding nearby. The Indian plan of killing was different from that used by the white man. The bulls usually lined the outside of the herd as a guard. The white man killed these and got questionable hides and meat. The Indians approached the herd and kept pace with it, shot down several bulls to make an opening, dashed their ponies through the breach, then killed cows, calves and two year olds. When their revolvers were empty or arrows gone, they gradually wormed their way out of the herd.

The Miamis killed more than 100 buffalo the first day. During the six weeks' hunt, they moved camp but once and then for only a few miles, as buffalo were constantly around them and water was abundant. They killed 1,700 buffaloes during the six weeks. The animals were skinned, the robes dried and tanned, and the hams cut into pieces similar to smoked beef. The rest of the animal was jerked, that is pulled off the carcass in thin strips and dried, after which it would keep for years.[6]

With the Omaha Indians on a Buffalo Hunt

When William Sternberg was Station Agent at Buffalo Station on the Kansas Pacific Railroad in 1873, he went with the Omaha Indians on a buffalo hunt. He wrote an account of his experiences on this hunt, as follows:

"Early in the month of November, I was somewhat startled at seeing a large band of Indians approaching from the north. There was no one at the station but the section men, Jim Thompson, and myself. Jim ran the boarding house.

"They proved to be peaceable Omaha Indians, under the leadership of their Chief 'Big Elk' on their annual buffalo hunt, in fact I think the whole tribe were there with the exception of a few old people left behind. They went into camp a short distance south of the station and it was an interesting sight to see with what skill and speed the squaws placed the tepee poles and covered them with their hide or canvas covering; a noisy village springing up like magic where a short hour before was naught but the solitary plains.

"The Indians hunt buffalo in their own peculiar way. They establish their camp in the buffalo country and then proceed to take it easy. The Chief designates men to act as scouts, and while men are loafing and horses resting in camp, it is their business to scout the surrounding country, locate the buffalo and ascertain the lay of the ground and how best to surround them.

"There were about 800 horses in the herd but only a comparatively small number were trained buffalo ponies, speedy enough to outrun the swiftest buffalo. These war ponies had the tip of their ears slit to designate them so that in the darkest night, if an emergency arose, they could quickly pick out the swiftest horses by feeling of their ears. For several days, the scouts failed to locate buffalo, and in the meantime I had gotten on friendly terms with Big Elk, and his sub-chief 'Yellow Smoke,' and a very intelligent young Indian named Frank La-Flesche who spoke excellent English, having been educated at the Agency school. At this time, I considered myself an expert checker player, had studied the most approved book-openings and many variations; but out of the many games played with Big Elk I never gained one, and consider him the finest player I ever met. I had, early in our acquaintance, asked him to allow me to accompany them on their first surround and he had consented on condition I should go unarmed, for he said his young men would not like me to participate in the killing as they wanted that sport and excitement for themselves. I was eager to go on any terms.

"On the morning of the fourth day, the camp was thrown into an uproar of excitement by the appearance of one of their scouts who, although a long distance from camp, by riding his horse in a certain manner conveyed to them the intelligence that he had located buffalo.

"The head man, in a powerful voice, was shouting orders. Some mounted and dashed away to drive in the horse herd, while others rushed around getting their equipment ready and by the time the scout had arrived seventy well-mounted Indians were ready to start. At the very first, Big Elk had sent me word to be ready if I wished to go with them, and I lost no time in saddling 'Doc' (dear old Doc, for nine years my constant companion and one of the fleetest horses on the plains). In a few minutes, we had started and for nearly twelve miles kept up a steady gallop, the horses were soon in a lather of sweat but the Indians showed them no mercy, which surprised me as I knew there was a sharp, fierce run yet to follow. After crossing the Saline River and going up the opposite slope nearly to the table land between the Saline and South Fork of the Solomon River, we suddenly drew rein, dismounted, and while Big Elk and the scout rode off, the Indians flinging themselves on the ground drew from arrow quivers at their backs, their long-stemmed red-clay pipes, and seemed to take great satisfaction in inhaling deeply and exhaling the smoke through the nose. The horses, after getting their breath, were permitted to graze. I took occasion at this time to notice their various arms. Most of them still used the bow and arrow, a few had Spencer rifles similar to those used by the United States Cavalry at that time. A few were armed, in addition to bows and arrows, with the old-fashioned cap and ball Colt's Dragoon pistols, while two of them carried long-barreled muzzle-loading Kentucky squirrel rifles. The arrows had one uniform groove along the shaft to designate the tribe, while each family had its particular tepee groove. These grooved arrows not only showed to which tepee the game belonged but made a channel for the blood to flow along freely which a smooth shaft would have prevented. After an absence of about an hour, Big Elk returned, and following his instructions, the men rapidly mounted and departed, some going westward and some to the east while Big Elk and the remainder, including myself, took it easy where we were. After what was to me an interminable wait, we suddenly noticed a column of smoke shoot up to the north almost directly opposite us, followed immediately by similar ones to the east and west of us. Big Elk had collected a few handsful of dry sage brush which he ignited and with a deft and peculiar twist of his blanket made a funnel which sent the thick smoke skyward in a straight column, then carefully stamping out the fire the order to mount was given.

"As we mounted the plateau, the Indians spread out fan-shaped to the right and left, and as we came over the crest of the divide, we saw the buffalo quietly lying down about a mile away. At the same moment, the Indians could be seen closing in from every direction, racing their horses at top speed and yelling like ten thousand demons. The startled buffalo knew not which way to turn for escape, and indeed there was no escape for them. In a moment, each buffalo was tearing across the plains in a mad dash for life, but there was an Indian for each buffalo, in fact there were seventy Indians and only sixty-five buffalo.

"Cody's Wild West show could not begin to offer the wild excitement that prevailed for the next half-hour. It was simply glorious. Frank La-Flesche, mounted on a magnificent rangy American horse, was the hero of the chase and killed five of the buffalo. It was a wonderful sight to see the Indians stripped to the waist and riding like centaurs, guiding their horses by their knees and the bending of their bodies, allowing free action of the arms to use the bow. They would shoot their arrows with such force that, missing a bone, it would go entirely through the body. For close range, I think they were as effective as the Colt's pistol which was the white man's chosen weapon for shooting buffalo from horseback.

"There were several tumbles occasioned by ponies putting a foot into a prairie dog hole, but the Indians ride with a long rawhide lariat fastened to the pony's under jaw which, passing under the left leg and beneath the girth, trails along behind; in case of a fall, this is seized before the pony gets beyond reach. Such a fall, so far as my experience goes, rarely results in serious injury to the rider, for although the horse may have been going at top speed the rider instinctively frees himself from the saddle and clears himself from the horse before the animal reaches the ground. The run over, the Indians gathered together laughing and chattering in great spirits, to my surprise paying no attention whatever to the dead buffalo, which was soon explained. It was for the squaws to attend to the drudgery, and soon a large number of them arrived from camp, many of their ponies dragging travois on which to carry the meat and hides. The travois were made from tent poles fastened on either side like a buggy-thills, except that one end drags upon the ground; just back of the pony's legs some cross pieces are fastened and a lace work of rawhide thongs made on which rests the load. I have seen expert butchers skinning cattle at slaughter houses but have never seen the work of the Indian squaws surpassed in this direction. They use a knife that has a thick blade, perfectly flat on one side and with a beveled edge on the other which greatly lessens the risk of cutting the hide.

"They had provided themselves with large quantities of small wooden pegs, and as soon as the hides were stripped off, small holes were cut around the edges and the hide was pegged to the ground stretched out to its fullest extent. Fleshing hoes were then used to remove all flesh, and indeed in case of the older animals the thickness of the skin was considerably reduced. After the hides were well dried, they were tied into compact bundles for transportation. The white buffalo-hunters wasted all the meat except the small amount they ate. The Indians saved everything. They cut the meat into long strips about an inch wide which is laid on the grass in the sun where it was quickly cured. The white man calls this 'jerked beef.'

"Every particle of the sinew was saved for thread and bow-strings. The Indians returned to camp later in the afternoon, but the squaws did not return until they had cured and bailed all the meat and hides which occupied them several days." [7]

Buffalo Drank the Solomon River Dry

Jeff Durfey, who was a professional buffalo hunter in the early days, killed thousands of the animals. At one time, he stood on the divide between the two Solomons and looked down on a solid mass of buffalo as far as he could see in all directions. He estimated that this herd was forty miles wide and he did not know how long. On another occasion, he camped on the bank of Beaver Creek which was six feet wide and six inches deep. A herd of buffalo came to the creek above the camp and drank it dry. The creek bed was dry for several hours. In 1872 a great herd drank the Solomon River dry; the water in it was twenty-five feet wide and a foot deep.[8]

How William F. Cody Acquired the Sobriquet "Buffalo Bill"

A pioneer newspaper published in Hays[9] contained an article on W. F. Cody's activities on the frontier in which the writer stated that the sobriquet was conferred on Cody in the following manner: "In 1867-8 he made his home in Hays and killed buffalo for a living and his frequent appearance on our streets peddling meat gained for him the name of Buffalo Bill."

The usual story is that the name, which Cody capitalized during his long career as a showman, was conferred on him while he was hunting buffalo to supply meat for the workmen who were building the Kansas Pacific Railroad west from Hays. The town site of Hays was laid out in June, 1867. The railroad reached the town site in October. Colonel Cody and his wife and little daughter Arta were living in the Perry House, the newly-built hotel on the north side of the railroad, when he made a contract with Goddard Brothers to supply the meat for the 1,200 workmen who were building the railroad west from town. It was estimated that an average of twelve animals a day would be required and Cody was to receive $500 a month for his work.

Cody was engaged as a hunter for the company for a period of less than eighteen months, during which time he killed 4,280 buffaloes. His equipment consisted of his trained buffalo horse named Brigham and "Lucretia Borgia," a newly improved, breech-loading needle gun which he had obtained from the Federal Government. Only the humps and hind quarters of the animals were used; the rest of the bodies, with the exception of the heads, were left to decay on the plains—an odorous reminder of that wanton slaughter of millions of these noble beasts within the short space of a few years. The heads were usually mounted by taxidermists, and for years adorned the offices of the Kansas Pacific Railroad and the lines which succeeded it.[10]

Cody's Defense of His New Title

The news that the name "Buffalo Bill" had been conferred on Cody reached the friends of William Comstock, chief of scouts at Fort Wallace, who was a successful buffalo hunter. They were indignant and demanded a buffalo-shooting contest between the two scouts for the title. The contest was to take place twenty miles east of Sheridan, and they were to hunt for eight hours one day. A wager of $500 was put up by each side. In his *Autobiography*,* Cody gives the following account of the event:

"The hunt took place twenty miles east of Sheridan. It had been well advertised, and there was a big 'gallery.' An excursion party, whose members came chiefly from St. Louis and numbered nearly a hundred ladies and gentlemen, came on a special train to view the sport. Among them was my wife and my little daughter Arta, who had come to visit me for a time.

"Buffaloes were plentiful. It had been agreed that we should go into the herd at the same time and make our 'runs,' each man killing as many animals as possible. A referee followed each of us on horseback, and counted the buffaloes killed by each man. The excursionists and other spectators rode out to the hunting-grounds in wagons and on horseback, keeping well out of sight of the buffaloes, so as not to frighten them

* Used by permission of Farrar and Rinehart, New York.

until the time came for us to dash into the herd. They were permitted to approach closely enough to see what was going on.

"For the first 'run' we were fortunate in getting good ground. Comstock was mounted on his favorite horse. I rode old Brigham. I felt confident that I had the advantage in two things: first, I had the best buffalo horse in the country; second, I was using what was known at the time as a needle-gun, a breech-loading Springfield rifle, caliber .50. This was 'Lucretia,' the weapon of which I have already told you. Comstock's Henry rifle, though it could fire more rapidly than mine, did not, I felt certain, carry powder and lead enough to equal my weapon in execution.

"When the time came to go into the herd, Comstock and I dashed forward, followed by the referees. The animals separated. Comstock took the left bunch, I the right. My great forte in killing buffaloes was to get them circling by riding my horse at the head of the herd and shooting their leaders. Thus the brutes behind were crowded to the left, so that they were soon going round and round.

"This particular morning, the animals were very accommodating. I soon had them running in a beautiful circle. I dropped them thick and fast till I had killed thirty-eight, which finished my 'run.'

"Comstock began shooting at the rear of the buffaloes he was chasing, and they kept on in a straight line. He succeeded in killing twenty-three, but they were scattered over a distance of three miles. The animals I had shot lay close together.

"Our St. Louis friends set out champagne when the result of the first run was announced. It proved a good drink on a Kansas prairie, and a buffalo hunter proved an excellent man to dispose of it.

"While we were resting we espied another herd approaching. It was a small drove, but we were prepared to make it serve our purpose. The buffaloes were cows and calves, quicker in their movements than the bulls. We charged in among them, and I got eighteen to Comstock's fourteen.

"Again the spectators approached, and once more the champagne went around. After a luncheon we resumed the hunt. Three miles distant we saw another herd. I was so far ahead of my competitor now that I thought I could afford to give an exhibition of my skill. Leaving my saddle and bridle behind, I rode, with my competitor, to windward of the buffaloes.

"I soon had thirteen down, the last one of which I had driven close to the wagons, where the ladies were watching the contest. It frightened some of the tender creatures to see a buffalo coming at full speed directly toward them, but I dropped him in his tracks before he had gotten within fifty yards of the wagon. This finished my 'run' with a score of sixty-nine buffaloes for the day. Comstock had killed forty-six.

"It was now late in the afternoon. Comstock and his backers gave up the idea of beating me. The referee declared me the winner of the match, and the champion buffalo hunter of the plains."

Matt Clarkson

Matt Clarkson was one of three brothers who hunted buffalo in western Kansas from 1867 to 1880. He and his brother George came from New York and arrived at Hays in July, 1867. Matt recorded part of his experiences and observations on writing pads and told others to William D. Philip. His account contains valuable information on the life and work of a buffalo hunter, and sidelights on conditions in and around Hays.[11]

The Clarkson brothers killed several thousand buffalo on the Saline and the Smoky Hill rivers in the fall of '67. They cut out the tongues and cut off the hams and left the remainder of the body. They saved every tongue, and in that way kept exact account of the number they killed. They owned three four-mule teams and two two-mule teams, so they could haul six to seven tons of meat at one time. As soon as they got two loads ready, they sent them to Hays so that the meat might be salted quickly. The work at the smoke-house kept George Clarkson occupied most of the time.

The brothers hunted on foot and preferred a low country. They killed from ten to forty animals in one place. The largest number Matt and his brother Charles killed at one time was fifty-four.

In August, 1868, they were camped at Spring Creek on the south side of the Smoky Hill. One night a band of Indians camped about a quarter of a mile below their camp. Unaware of their presence, the hunters set out the following morning, and when they returned, they found that the Indians had taken their grub, blankets, a mule, and most everything else. Charlie Clarkson had to go to Hays and purchase four hundred dollars worth of new equipment and provisions. They vowed that, if they ever saw the red skins again, blood would be spilled.

The number of buffalo killed by the brothers is recorded in the manuscript. In September, 1872, Clarkson was camping on the Smoky Hill and was killing for the hides which were worth $3.50 a piece. By the 20th of that month, he had sold hides from that camp amounting to $4,550. In October they moved to Ladder Creek where the buffaloes were numerous and "not very wild." It was not much of a job to kill all they could skin; they aimed to skin from 140 to 200 animals a day. The entry on October 20 reads as follows:

"We have named this Ladder Creek camp the 'Slaughter Pen.' In all we have killed about 7,000 buffalo in the camp."

Five days later, he says that they killed 1,300 buffaloes and hauled them to Wallace. Then they moved the camp about

thirty miles north where they killed about 2,400 buffaloes and
a number of antelope. In December they camped on the Republican, and in thirty days killed 800 of the beasts.

During the time the Clarkson brothers were at Rome, they
killed 22,000 buffaloes.

Sidelights on the Royal Hunt

Grand Duke Alexis of Russia and his party arrived at
North Platte, Nebraska, January 13, 1872. With secretaries,
valets and servants, the retinue was large. Among the Ameri-
cans, who accompanied the royal party, were Generals Philip
H. Sheridan, James W. Forsyth, George A. Forsyth, and
George A. Custer. General Innis N. Palmer, Colonel W. F.
(Buffalo Bill) Cody, and a number of other officers and
gentlemen met the party at North Platte. They started immediately on the trip to the camp, perhaps fifty miles distant,
where experienced plainsmen, hunters, and guides had been
gathered.

Among the scouts, who participated in the royal hunt, was
Amos Cole, generally known as "Ame" Cole. He came to
Kansas at an early date as a government scout and was well
known in northwestern Kansas, Nebraska, and Colorado. He
was a physical giant and was a great walker. Cole often
walked from his farm on the Prairie Dog to Phillipsburg, fifty
miles distant, returning the next day with a forty-eight pound
sack of flour on his shoulder.

During the royal hunt, the camp accoutrement was extremely primitive. One meal the bill of fare was biscuits and
gravy. Table appointments were "a la naturale." There was
one basin which held the gravy. There were no knives, forks,
spoons or plates. Each man took a biscuit in his hand and all
ate gravy from the common bowl. Grand Duke Alexis,
whose appetite was heightened by hard riding and the high

altitude, dipped his biscuit into the gravy, took a bite, and dipped again, oblivious of others. Ame Cole, regardless of rank, instructed the Duke that a more sanitary way could be managed just as easily by breaking off one bite of biscuit at a time and dipping it in the gravy. It is not recorded how the royal visitor took the rebuke.[12]

The writers on the royal buffalo hunt state that the party left Camp Alexis for the train at North Platte early in the morning of January 16, left for Cheyenne that evening, and reached Denver two days later. In the evening of the 19th, the party started east over the Kansas Pacific Railroad, stopping at Kit Carson for another buffalo hunt. During the night of January 21, the special train steamed through Kansas and arrived at Topeka the following morning.[13]

An item in the Ellsworth *Reporter* that week corroborates their accounts. It reads as follows:

"Duke Alexis did himself the honor to pass through Ellsworth the other night sleeping in seven palace cars. He did not call at the *Reporter* office and we don't care, it will be a good excuse for us not calling on him when we go to Russia."

There is a tradition in Ellsworth that Grand Duke Alexis visited that community in the early days. Most everyone who has resided there for any length of time has heard the story. One version says that Buffalo Bill Cody and Archibald Forbes, correspondent of the London *Times*, accompanied the Duke on this trip. According to another version, the Grand Duke's party passed through Ellsworth in 1872, as stated above, but stopped at Fort Harker.

The writer has been unable to locate any contemporaneous documents on this visit. The best evidence has been supplied by two pioneer residents of Ellsworth, namely, Ed. Schermerhorn, who lives at Wilson, Kansas, and Lenas Stein, who died recently in Wyoming. Mr. Schermerhorn says that the Grand Duke came to Fort Harker, but that he was there in

1867, not in 1872. He was a clerk in the Sutler's store at Harker at the time and remembers selling liquor to the Duke at the bar. Mr. Stein states that the Grand Duke "was here to hunt buffalo, but the herds had been driven farther west by the continuous slaughter for hides, so he went to Fort Hays, where he was given an escort from the post, as the Indians were on the warpath at the time."

Ellsworth folk say that the Grand Duke and Cody visited the scene of Colonel Henry Inman's well-known story "The Ranche on the Oxhide" while the royal party was at Fort Harker. The visitors carved their names on a rock which still stands in Vance's pasture about a mile and a half south of Ellsworth, and has been known as Alexis Rock. At some time, the date 1872 was carved below their names. Mr. Stein recalls that he came upon the party when the Duke was carving his name. Several years ago, a picture of the rock showing the names and the date appeared in print.[14] During the intervening years, the rock has been beaten by the weather and stock have rubbed against it. A large piece, where the name "Will Cody" and the date were carved beneath the Grand Duke's name, has been broken off. Of the original inscription, only the words "Alexis Duke" remain.

Buffalo Hunt Along the Kansas Pacific

On October 2, 1868, De B. Randolph Keim left Hays on a Kansas Pacific train for Sheridan located at the end of the track. As already stated, about thirty miles west of Hays immense herds of buffaloes were seen. Several animals were shot from the cars. The train stopped so that a few "rumps" might be brought in. While this was being done, Keim and six or seven others started down the track to dispatch a buffalo which had been wounded. When the party got within fifty yards, a shot was fired at the animal which seemed to have a vitalizing effect. With a desperate effort the beast regained his feet and made for the men head down, tongue out, bleeding and frothing at the mouth, eyes flashing, and bellowing loudly. Keim ran across the track and into the ditch on the other side. The rest of the party followed him.

Losing sight of the hunters, the enraged animal gave vent to his anger upon the opposite side of the railroad embankment by rending great furrows in the earth, stamping the ground, and making a terrible noise. Three of the men raised up to get a partial sight of his body not over thirty feet away and fired, the rest holding in reserve. Every ball seemed to take effect. The beast fell upon his knees. The rest then fired and he rolled completely over. His tenacity of life was remarkable. He must have had a dozen bullets in his body. Notwithstanding this, he struggled until he again got on his feet. He could not walk but stood, moving his head to the right and left, and glaring defiantly at the men while streams of blood ran from his nostrils. Repeated shots were fired into his body. As each ball entered, the only visible effect was a slight turn of the head and swish of the tail. At length, after having been literally peppered with lead, a sudden quiver passed over his entire body and he staggered and fell dead.[15]

A Buffalo Hunt Near Hays

A short time after W. E. Webb of Topeka and his party of sportsmen arrived at Hays in the fall of '69, they started for the Saline to hunt buffalo. The course which they followed lay a little west of north. Some distance out the attention of the party was directed to a dark mass of moving objects a mile away upon their right. The Mexicans in the party pronounced them buffaloes. Dobeen, the cook, asked permission to pursue the animals and, getting astride a donkey, was off at a gallop. Man and mule soon disappeared in a ravine which seemed to wind almost into the midst of the herd. At length, they saw him riding gallantly out of the ravine for a charge. A few moments later game and hunter were face to face. Just then one of the party ejaculated.

"As I am alive Dobeen's coming this way, at a bloody good run and the buffalo after him!"

Sure enough pursuer and pursued had changed places. The game, however, was rapidly changing in appearance and suddenly spread out into a fan-like shape and the spectators all cried simultaneously,

"Indians!"

The whole outfit now whirled about and was headed toward Hays. Two of the horses ran away, which started a general stampede among the other horses. About this time, the Indians stopped running and stood in a dusky line about a half-mile away, making signs to the whites. The guide, who had stayed with the wagons, motioned to the horsemen to return.

By the time the cook rode up out of breath and perspiring terribly, two savages had ridden out from their band weaponless and gestured a wish to communicate. Two of Webb's men rode out to meet them.

The Indians proved to be a band of Cheyennes, under White Wolf, or, as he was more frequently called, Medicine Wolf, straight as an arrow and developed like a giant. The Whites had no difficulty in understanding that the Indians were hungry and wished something to eat. As the hunters had only a few provisions, but did not dare to refuse the savages, they invited them to accompany the party back to Hays. The red skins accepted the invitation and they were soon retracing their steps to the frontier town.

As the strange cavalcade entered Hays, the people came out to meet them. The news reached the Fort and some officers rode over. The Land Company's office was selected for a council room, the Cheyennes tying their ponies to the stage corral nearby. The postmaster of Hays, Jim Hall, acted as interpreter. One of the Indians took from a sack a red clay pipe with a long bowl and inserted into it a three-foot stem profusely ornamented with brass tacks and a tassel of painted horse hair. This was handed to White Wolf, together with a small bag of tobacco. The Chief took a few puffs, emitting the fumes with a hoarse blowing like a miniature steam-engine. Then he passed the pipe along and it commenced its journey around the room. After some speech-making by Chief White Wolf and other leaders, the council broke up.

One of the sporting party, who took notes, rendered White Wolf's speech at the council in verse as follows:

> White brother, have pity; the White Wolf is poor,
>   The skin of his belly is shrunk to his back;
> A gallon of whisky is good for a cure,
>   If followed by plenty of "bacon and tack."
>
> The red man is noble, big Injun is me:
>   Like berries all crimson and ready to pick,
> The scalps on my pole are a heap good to see—
>   Good medicine they when poor Injun is sick.
>
> The red man is truth, and the white one is lies;
>   The first suffers wrong at the hand of the other;
> The way they skin us is good for sore eyes,
>   The way we skin them, astonishing, rather.
>
> They rob us of guns and offer us plows,
>   And tell us to farm it, to go into corn;
> We're good to raise hair, and good to raise rows,
>   And good to raise essence of corn—in a horn.
>
> Go back to your cities and leave us our home,
>   Or off with your scalp and that remnant of shirt;
> Go, let the poor Injun in happiness roam,
>   And live on his buffalo, puppies, and dirt.

The Indians got hold of some liquor and soon became drunk. Two or three of them mounted their ponies and prepared for a race through the streets. At the lower end of the street they got as nearly in line as their inebriated condition would permit and when the word was given, started off with loud shouts. The animal that came out ahead had no rider to claim the honors, the jockey having fallen off midway, and was sitting on the ground looking the wrong way down the track. White Wolf and two of his braves then gave a display of their skill in the use of their bows, shooting at a stake sixty yards off. The Indians were given food; their eating powers were marvelous. The chief, inside of two hours, devoured three hearty meals.

Their entertainment at the town being concluded, the Indians were conducted over to the Fort where some rations were given them. They manifested a fondness for sugar but took anything, in fact everything, they could get. They came back through town, and promising peace, departed across the plains.[16]

Witches on the Plains

On the first evening of their homeward journey from Sheridan, W. E. Webb and his party camped on what appeared to be a small tributary of the Upper Solomon. While the tents were being pitched and the provisions unloaded, one of the men strolled toward a clump of trees half a mile off, hoping to secure a wild turkey. He soon came running back in great fright to tell the others that, as he was passing among the trees, the black pacer of the plains with its bloody master in the saddle had started out of a bottom meadow just beyond and fled away into the gloom. As he turned to flee, he saw a hideous Indian witch swinging to and fro in a tree directly before him.

Six members of the party started out to investigate, fearing that Indians might be lurking in the vicinity. They soon reached the timber, and as they walked forward the witch suddenly appeared before them. It was the body of a dead papoose fastened in a tree. The spot was evidently an Indian burying-ground. The corpse has been loosened by the wind and now rocked back and forth staring at them. It was dried into a shriveled deformity rendered doubly grotesque by the beads and other articles with which it had been decked when laid away.[17]

Fight With a Buffalo

On June 13, 1876, H. C. Allen of Hays and W. N. Morphy, who had removed from Hays to Dodge City, had a fight with a good-sized buffalo calf. The men were driving over the prairie between Buckner and Saw Log when they saw a herd of buffalo approaching. The only weapons in their possession were a .32 caliber revolver and a ripping knife. Morphy jumped on his pony with the revolver and struck out for the game; Allen following with the ripping knife as soon as he could detach one of his horses from the wagon. Morphy singled out a buffalo and fired at him five times, but the pony jumped down in such a position that not one of the shots took effect. Soon getting tired of running, the animal turned and charged the pony. He charged several times when the pony turned on the buffalo. They collided; pony, buffalo and Morphy were scattered on the ground. All three regained their footing at the same time and each commenced business; the buffalo to butting the pony and Morphy to kicking the buffalo. The buffalo, turning quickly, made for Morphy. The latter seized him around the neck and they went to the ground together, the man uppermost. Just at this time, Allen arrived, and while the bison was down, thrust his knife into its vitals, thus ending one of the most unique struggles ever heard of outside of a ten cent novel.[18]

A Detroiter's First Hunt

A newspaper correspondent from Detroit, on his way home from a trip in the far West in the fall of 1871, stopped for a day or two at O'Fallen's, Nebraska. A party, composed of Captain James Egan and Lieutenant J. L. Fowler of the Second United States Cavalry; E. O. Earle of the Union Pacific Railroad; and nine others, were ready to set out on a buffalo hunt and invited the Detroiter to accompany them.

They rode for about three hours before striking the range. At length, they sighted the sentinels of the herd and made offensive preparations at once. Each man carried a good rifle and a revolver. These were gotten ready for action. The newspaperman was new at this sport and his hands shook so that he could scarcely hold his rifle. They crept their horses slowly forward and were well on the herd before being discovered. Then there was a confused bellowing and away went the herd.

"Forward boys!" shouted the captain. Every man gave his horse the spurs and dashed among the buffalo. The reporter sought to manage his excited steed with one hand and fire his rifle with the other. Consequently, the first shot was thrown away as the horse plunged and leaped among the shaggy monsters. Then the rider let his horse take care of himself, while he aimed and brought down a young cow.

The party drove back a number of the herd in order to give the Detroiter all honor possible, and again he killed a buffalo. Then they set out in quest of further adventure. The hunters now made several valuable suggestions—such as telling the Easterner to back up his horse and let him kill the buffalo with his heels.

The correspondent made a dash for a shaggy old bull, which stood gazing at the men in sullen defiance. Riding up within a dozen rods of the animal, he sent a bullet against his cast-iron head when the old monarch came at the man. Away went horse and rider at topmost speed. After chasing them for about forty rods, the shaggy monster checked his speed. Then the Detroiter rode around the buffalo in circles, keeping far enough away to be prepared for a charge, and sent bullet after bullet into him until he reeled, swayed to and fro for a moment, and then went down.[19]

A Day on Big Creek

In August, 1871, a party consisting of Messrs. Keim, General Ticket Agent of the Kansas Pacific Railroad, J. D. Marston, agent of that railroad, and E. St. Johns, General Ticket Agent of the Rock Island; Major Robinson and Lieutenant Baldwin of Fort Hays; and Dennis Ryan of Hays City, started from Hays for a day's hunt. They struck off to the south, camping near the confluence of the Smoky Hill and Big Creek. They sighted three large buffaloes there, but after a long chase, they returned to camp. Then they followed the course of the creek about five miles where they found a large herd. Two animals were killed. Several exciting chases took place, in which Mr. Ryan and Major Robinson especially distinguished themselves.

The hunters, after partaking of well-earned refreshments, left the trail in pursuit of another herd. Keim, mounted on Major Robinson's famous buffalo horse, singled out a mighty bull and pursued him in hot haste. In the chase, he lost his hat and revolver. Without the assistance of weapons, he succeeded, however, in driving the game home where he was dispatched.

The day was drawing to a close, so the party decided to return to Hays, highly satisfied with the results of the hunt; they had killed six monarchs of the prairie. They took luncheon with the veteran Jack Callahan who was the accustomed dater for the heroes of the chase. Then they climbed into the military vehicle provided by Major Robinson and set out for home. The toils of the day did not dampen the spirit of St. Johns who continued to shoot at the quails and turtle-doves on the homeward journey and made his advent into Hays waving triumphantly two buffalo tails which he had captured. The remainder of the party were glad of an opportunity to repose quietly in the vehicle which presented more the appearance of a sleeping car than a military buggy.[20]

Storms

Mrs. Anna Campbell Boston, whose parents, Mr. and Mrs. Perry Campbell, settled on Thompson Creek in Ellsworth County in 1866, says,[21]

"In the fall of the year the men of our little community would gather together and go buffalo hunting and secure meat for our winter supply. On one occasion when my father was one of the number, the hunters were lost in a blizzard and were unable to find their way; they were several days without food excepting the flesh of a wild cat they had luckily caught. The storm was severe and they could not tell where they were or what direction to go, so decided to let the faithful oxen guide them, with a team of horses following, and were not long in reaching my uncle's home on Thompson Creek after having been given up as lost by the women and children."

Early in March, 1867, a party of four old buffalo hunters were camped in the Paradise valley, then a famous rendezvous of the animals they were after. One day when they were out on the range stalking, and widely separated from each other, a terrible blizzard came up. Three of the hunters reached their camp without much difficulty, but he who was farthest away was caught in it, when night overtook him. Fortunately, he soon came up with a super annuated bull that had been abandoned by the herd; he killed him, took out his viscera and crawled inside the empty carcass, where he lay comparatively comfortable until morning, when the storm passed over and the sun shone brightly. But when he attempted to get out, he found himself a prisoner, the immense ribs of the creature having frozen together, and locked him up as tightly as if he were in a cell. Fortunately his companions, who were searching for him, and firing their rifles from time to time, heard him yell in response to the discharge of their pieces, and thus discovered and released him from the peculiar predicament into which he had fallen.[22]

A curious incident occurred along the Kansas Pacific Railroad during a severe storm in the winter of 1870-71. The train was stopped while the storm raged, and a large number of buffaloes congregated around the train, standing on the leeside for protection.[23]

In January, 1874, Joe Bernard and a man named Vansicle, while hunting buffalo on the prairie south of Dodge, were overtaken by one of those severe snow and wind storms which, at that season of the year, frequently visited the plains. The two men wandered about for some time until they finally became separated. Vansicle found his way to camp in a badly frozen condition, but young Bernard was not heard of afterwards. In the summer of 1879, while Johnny Berkley and Charley Todd were returning over the country from the south and were crossing the head waters of Crooked Creek, thirty-five miles southwest of Dodge, they discovered a human skeleton. Near the skeleton was one boot and a short clay pipe such as was possessed by Bernard when last seen. From the locality, circumstances, etc., there was no doubt that the skeleton was that of Joe Bernard.[24]

The Wild Huntress

The Indians were especially troublesome around Hays in 1867. In May of that year, the Lookout stage station, six miles southwest of town, was raided by the Indians and four men were killed and scalped. Later in the year, six section hands on the Kansas Pacific Railroad were killed and scalped near Victoria, and were buried at the North Fork Crossing of Big Creek. A railroad laborer was also killed a short distance west of Hays. A contractor, living in a dugout not far from town, was shot with an arrow through a knot hole in the plank door. His wife, who witnessed the murder, went insane and rode about the country on a black mustang seeking revenge, a terror to the superstitious red skins, though she was not certain whether the murderer was a Cheyenne or a white man with whom her husband had quarreled and fought. She spent much of her time riding after buffaloes and firing a revolver at them in an aimless sort of way. She got into print as the "Wild Huntress of the Plains."

W. E. Webb of Topeka and his party of scientists and sportsmen met her on the plains while they were going from Silver Creek to Sheridan. Webb tells about this meeting in his book *Buffalo Land*, as follows:

"The second day after leaving Silver Creek, we suddenly encountered another specialty of the plains, the 'Wild Huntress.' So often has this personage and her male counterpart danced, with big letters and a bowie-knife, across yellow covers, that we met the 'original Jacobs' of the tribe gleefully. She came to us in a cloud of buffalo, with black eyes glittering like a snake's, and coarse and uncombed hair that tangled itself in the wind and streamed and twisted behind her like withering vipers. A black riding habit flowed out in the strong breeze, its train snapping like a loose sail, and a black mustang fled from her Indian lash—the dark wild horse, a fit carrier for such somber outfit.

"She was introduced to us by the bison herd, which came thundering across our front, with this strange figure pressing its flank and darting hither and thither from one outskirt of the flying multitude to the other. The reins lay loose on the neck of her mustang, which entered into the fierce chase like a bloodhound, doubling and twisting on its course with an agility that was wonderful.

"One hand of the huntress held out a holster revolver, which she fired occasionally, but with an uncertain aim, one of the bullets indeed whistling our way. The chase consti-tuted the excitement that she sought, and the pistol was little more than a spur to urge it on.

" 'That's Ann, poor P—'s wife,' said our guide. 'Crazy since the Indians killed her husband. He was a contractor on the railroad; his camp used to be just above Hays. She lives in the old "dug-out" on the line yet, and spends half her time chasing buffalo. She never kills none; but that isn't what she is after. She wants to be moving, and just as wild as she can; it sort o' relieves her mind.'

"The huntress had seen our outfit, and rode toward us. The face was a very plain one, with a vacant yet anxious expres-sion, and the tightly-drawn skin seeming scarcely to cover the jaw-bones. She halted before us, and commenced conver-sation at once.

" 'Good day, gentlemen.'

" 'Good day, Madam.'

" 'She always tells her story to everybody,' muttered the guide in a low voice.

" 'Have you seen any Cheyennes hereabouts, gentlemen? I

sighted a party this morning, and you ought to have seen them run. Raven Dick, here, put his best foot foremost, but they shook him out of sight in a ravine. Haven't anything better to do, friends, and so I'm riding down some buffalo.'

"We could easily understand why superstitious savages should run when a maniac female of such dismal aspect flitted along their trail.

" 'Out from Hays, sirs?' she continued, after a pause. 'I left there yesterday. Dick and I camped last night. We must be home when the men come in from work this eve. Up, Rave!' and she struck the mustang a cruel blow, from which he jumped with quivering muscles, only to be violently curbed. For the first time she had just noticed our guide, and sat for an instant with her wild eyes eating a way to his heart. Then she turned again to us.

" 'Sirs, you must aid me. Some say the Cheyennes killed my husband, and others there be who think Abe there did it. More shame to me who has to tell it, but the two had a fight about a woman, some months gone. It was just after pay-day, and husband was drunk; otherwise he'd never have bothered his head about any girl but the one he married.

" 'There were blows and black eyes, and being a rough man's quarrel, it ended with hand-shaking. My man came home, and we sat by the fire that night, and I took no notice that he'd been wrong, but spoke of our old home in Ohio, and asked him wouldn't he go back there when the contract was finished. And he put his hand on mine, and says: "Sis, if the cuts and fills on the next mile work to profit, we'll go home." Just then there came a hiss from the door at our backs, and husband turned sharp and quick. There was a knot hole in the planks, and its round black mouth, gaping from out in the night at us, had spit the sound into our ears. Husband he rose and went to the door, and fell back dying, with an arrow in his breast. Some said it was a Cheyenne, and others said Abe did it. There were lots of Indian bows in camp, and Cheyennes don't kill for the love of it, but only to steal. I'm going to ask them, if I can catch them, did they do it, and if not I know who did. I've a bow, Abe, and an arrow too, and I hope his blood isn't on your hands.'

" 'I didn't do it, Ann. I don't shoot no man in the dark,' replied our hostler guide, with a sullen defiance, which among that class stands equally well for innocence or guilt. We looked at the two, as they sat for an instant facing each other. The picture was a weird one—a wildcat, fronting the object of its chase, but undecided whether to spring or not. We felt that the dark maniac had been hovering around us, and that this meeting was not altogether accidental. Her disordered brain was yet undecided in which direction vengeance lay, and, like a tigress, she was watching and waiting."

Songs of the Range

The hunters on the buffalo range included men who had received a classical education, as well as the illiterate type. Several of the better educated were good writers and left valuable accounts of their experiences in the buffalo country. Others wrote verse; in this class was Harry Burns, a Scotch-Englishman, said to have been a descendant of the famous Scotch bard. One of his poems, published in the Dodge City *Times*, was addressed to the "hunters after the ninety days' scout" in Texas in 1877. A song entitled "The Buffalo Hunter," by "Rambling Jim" and "respectfully ascribed to Harry Baker" was published in the *Ford County Globe*, August 27, 1878. According to John R. Cook, author of *The Border and The Buffalo*, a hunter, whose parents were well-to-do, composed a song when he was leaving western Kansas to hunt in Texas. The words were sung all over the range with as much vim as the old-time John Brown song. It was set to a catchy tune, and with the melody from the hunters' voices it was beautiful and soul-inspiring.[25] The song is known at present as "A Home on the Range." A recent law suit over the authorship of this song has brought to light the information that Dr. Brewster Higley, who homesteaded on Beaver Creek in Smith County, Kansas, in the early '70s, wrote a poem entitled "A Western Home" in 1873, which was printed in the *Smith County Pioneer* the same year. It is claimed that this was the original version of the song.

Notes .

Chapter One: THE WAGON TRAILS

1. Blackmar, *Kansas, a Cyclopedia of State History*, II, 736. This source has been used for other general information on the trails and stage lines. Root and Connelley, *The Overland Stage to California* also used for general information.
2. The copy of this paper is on file in the Kansas Historical Society Library and has been quoted by writers on the Santa Fe Trail.
3. *Rocky Mountain News*, May 14, 1859.
4. *Ibid.*, May 7, 1859.
5. Atchison *Weekly Free Press*, October 5, 1865.
6. *Rocky Mountain News*, May 31 and June 7, 1865.
7. *Ibid.*, July 5, 1865.
8. Adapted from Account by A. L. Carpenter, stage driver, written for the Kansas City *Star*, Green Scrapbook, No. 47, p. 275.
9. *Daily Rocky Mountain News*, December 1 and 4, 1865.
10. Report of Major General P. H. Sheridan, 1868, in U.S. War Department, *Report of the Secretary of War*, 1868-69.

11. Bowles, *Across the Continent*, 15-16; Richardson, *Beyond the Mississippi*, 327-329.

12. Junction City *Union*, March 14, 1868.

13. Greeley, *Overland Journey to California in 1859*, 20ff.; Lawrence *Republican*, May 26, 1859; Richardson, *Beyond the Mississippi*, 161 ff.

14. Root and Connelley, *The Overland Stage to California*, 559-560.

15. Accounts of these record-breaking rides contained in Bowles, *Across the Continent;* Richardson, *Beyond the Mississippi;* and other sources.

16. Jefferson *Inquirer*, January 22, March 25, June 3, September 30, 1848; *Missouri Statesman*, June 9, 1848. Hays *Daily News*, November 17, 1931 reprinting a popular article by J. Frank Dobie, in New York *Herald Tribune Magazine*, Sunday, July 5, 1931. Root and Connelley, *The Overland Stage to California;* Alexander Majors, *Seventy Years on the Frontier;* Richardson, *Beyond the Mississippi;* and other writers tell about this ride. William R. Bernard's article in Kansas State Historical Society, *Collections*, IX, 552, has been used for information on Aubry's death. About 1879 a postoffice called Zamore was established near Aubrey. In 1885 the names Aubrey and Zamore were dropped and the name Kendall chosen.

17. Bradley, *The Story of the Pony Express;* Root and Connelley, *The Overland Stage to California;* Chapman, *The Pony Express;* articles in the Kansas City *Star;* and other sources.

18. Lawrence *Republican*, April 26, 1860.

19. Greeley: *Overland Journey to California*, 47-48.

20. New York *Daily Tribune*, November 9, 1854.

21. Greene, *The Kansas Region*, 113.

22. *Rocky Mountain News*, May 2, 1866.

23. Atchison *Daily Globe*, 1910 and 1925; Andreas, *History of Kansas;* and some of the county histories contain information on Mormon Grove.

24. Greene, *The Kansas Region*, 26-28.

25. Based on Majors, *Seventy Years on the Frontier.*

26. Adapted from Root and Connelley, *Overland Stage*, 560-562.

27. Kansas City *Journal of Commerce* in late '6os and '7os tells about snake hunts.
28. Max Greene, Henry Inman, and other writers give accounts of The Caches.
29. Dodge City *Times*, September 22, 1877.
30. Young, *Dangers of the Trail*, 21-25, contains a good description of bull whackers.
31. Kansas City *Star*, January 9, 1927.
32. Webb, *Buffalo Land*, 143.

Chapter Two: THE CATTLE TRAILS

1. McCoy, *Historic Sketches of the Cattle Trade*, 52.
2. Topeka *Commonwealth*, August 15, 1871. The figures were supplied by Joseph G. McCoy who includes same figures in his book.
3. Joseph Nimmo, "The Range and Ranch Cattle Traffic," U.S. 48th Congress. 2nd Session. *House Executive Document* 267. Mr. Nimmo was Chief of the Bureau of Statistics, Treasury Department, and made his report in 1885.
4. Kansas City *Daily Journal of Commerce*, March 25, 1871; Scribner's *Monthly* quoted in *Ellis County Star*, March 11, 1880; McCoy, *Historic Sketches of the Cattle Trade;* Everett Dick, "The Long Drive," in Kansas State Historical Society, *Collections*, XVII.
5. Wichita City Council, *Proceedings*, 1871 (manuscript); Wichita *Eagle*, May 21, 1874.
6. Figures taken from contemporary files of Abilene *Chronicle;* Topeka *Commonwealth;* and Kansas City *Daily Journal of Commerce.*
7. N. Y. *Sun* quoted in *Thomas County Cat*, April 1, 1886; Kansas City *Daily Journal of Commerce*, April 23, 1871.
8. Wichita *Eagle*, June 14, 1872; New York *Sun* quoted in *Thomas County Cat*, April 1, 1886.
9. Kansas City *Daily Journal of Commerce*, April 23, 1871.
10. Scribner's *Monthly*, quoted in Ellis County *Star*, March 11, 1880; Kansas City *Daily Journal of Commerce.*

11. Junction City *Union*, February 26, 1870; Topeka *Daily Commonwealth*, June 28, 1871; Kansas City *Daily Journal of Commerce*, July 9, 1871.

12. McCoy, *Historic Sketches of the Cattle Trade*, 63-65.

13. Ellsworth *Reporter*, March 14, 1872.

14. Blanchard, *Conquest of Southwest Kansas*, 58.

15. *Ibid.*, 76.

Chapter Three: THE KANSAS COW TOWNS

1. The following sources were used in gathering the stories of Abilene: Abilene *Chronicle*, 1870-71; Cheyenne, Wyoming, *Leader*, 1868; Junction City *Union;* Kansas City *Star;* Topeka *Commonwealth; Human Life; the Magazine About People*, 1907; Abilene City Council Minutes, 1870-72; papers in State of Kansas vs. Andrew McConnell and Moses Miles, District Court of Riley County, 1870-71; U.S. Census Bureau. Schedules for 1870 (Manuscript); personal interviews with J. B. Edwards and Homer Wilson, two pioneer residents; John Wesley Hardin, *Autobiography;* Walton, *Life and Adventures of Ben Thompson;* McCoy, *Historic Sketches of the Cattle Trade;* Theodore C. Henry, Address on Abilene and Thomas James Smith under title, "Two City Marshals," in Kansas Historical Society, *Collections*, IX, 526-540; and accounts of the murder of Marshal Tom Smith in Stuart Henry, *Conquering the Great American Plains;* Andreas, *History of Kansas*.

2. For Ellsworth: Ellsworth County Coroner's papers in the inquest on the bodies of Sheriff Whitney and Ed Crawford; State of Kansas versus William Thompson, District Court of Ellsworth County, 1873-77; Ellsworth City Police Court Records, 1871-74 (Judge Osborne's court); Ellsworth City Council Minutes, 1871-74; Ellsworth *Reporter; Saline County Journal;* Junction City *Union*, Hays *Sentinel*, Topeka *Commonwealth*, and other newspapers; State Archives, Topeka, Kansas; Rangers Papers in Texas Archives; personal inter-

views with the following eye-witnesses: John Montgomery,
Ernest Cunningham, Ed Schermerhorn, Charles Larkin. The
story of the shooting of Sheriff Whitney has also been gotten
from other eye-witnesses through a third party, and from
those who have heard eye-witnesses, now dead, tell the
story many times on the streets and in the homes of Ellsworth.
Published with changes in *The Aerend*, Vol. V, Nos. 2 and 3.

3. For Newton: Newton City Council Minutes, 1872-73; and
Ordinance Book; Newton *Kansan*, 1872-73; Wichita *Eagle*,
1872; Ellsworth *Reporter* 1872; Kansas City *Daily Journal
of Commerce*, 1871; Abilene *Chronicle*, 1871; Kansas City
Star, 1925; Topeka *State Record*, 1872; Topeka *Commonwealth*, 1871; R.W.P. Muse "History of Harvey County,
Kansas" in *Arkansas Valley Democrat*, June 1, 1883; Letters
from and personal interviews with Henry Brunner of Fitzgerald, Georgia, who came to Newton on May 19, 1871 and
was proprietor of the Santa Fe Hotel and in other business
for many years; and with H. W. Prouty who settled northwest of Newton, August 29, 1871, and still resides on his
homestead.

4. For Wichita: Wichita *Eagle*, 1872-75, 1926, 1931; Wichita
Beacon, 1874-75; Wichita *Vidette*, 1870; Kansas City *Journal
of Commerce*, 1871; Ellsworth *Reporter*, 1873; Harper's
Weekly, 1874; Wichita City Council, Minutes, 1870-75;
Wichita City Council, Ordinance Book; Wichita City Clerk.
Ledger, 1874; Warrant Record, 1874-75; Bently, *History of
Wichita and Sedgwick County, Kansas*; Andreas, *History of
Kansas*.

5. For Dodge City: Dodge City *Times*, 1876-78; *Ford County
Globe*, 1878-85; *Ellis County Star*, 1876-82; Hays *Sentinel*,
1876-79; Dodge City *Cowboy*; Ellsworth *Reporter*, 1874;
Dodge City, City Council, Ordinance Book; Kansas State
Census, 1875 (Manuscript); Letters from Thomas Masterson,
Wichita; and Merritt L. Beeson, Dodge City; Wright, *Dodge
City, The Cowboy Capital*; Eddie Foy, *Clowning Through
Life*; Siringo, *The Lone Star Cowboy*; Hunter, *The Trail
Drivers of Texas*; Merritt Beeson, leaflet on Boot Hill.

Chapter Four: THE BUFFALO RANGE

1. Keim, *Sheridan's Troopers on the Borders*, 38.
2. Cody, *Autobiography*, 82.
3. Inman, *The Old Santa Fe Trail*, 204-205.
4. Quoted in Kansas City *Daily Journal of Commerce*, August 17, 1869.
5. Hays *Daily News*, November 30, 1933.
6. Ely Moore, "A Buffalo Hunt with the Miamis, in 1854," Kansas State Historical Society, *Collections*, X, 402-07.
7. From a manuscript in the possession of Frank Sternberg, San Francisco, California.
8. Kansas City *Star* (Sunday), May 28, 1911, p. 10 A.
9. Hays *Sentinel*, January 26, 1877.
10. Mrs. Cody, *Memories of Buffalo Bill*, 109; Cody, *Autobiography;* Helen Cody Wetmore's book; and other sources contain the story of the origin of the name Buffalo Bill.
11. The manuscript copy of the Matt Clarkson Diary.
12. Story contributed by Miss Helen Malcolm, Almena, Kansas.
13. Kansas City *Daily Journal of Commerce*, January 14-23, 1872; accounts by James A. Hadley and C. M. Beeson in Kansas State Historical Society, *Collections*, Vol. X.
14. Clipping in Scrapbook No. 24, p. 778, Charles R. Green Collection, Fort Hays Kansas State College Library.
15. Keim, *Sheridan's Troopers on the Borders*, 38-40.
16. Adapted from Webb, *Buffalo Land*, 154-179.
17. *Ibid.*, 389-390.
18. *Ellis County Star*, June 15, 1876.
19. Detroit *Daily Free Press*, Supplement, October 16, 1871.
20. Kansas City *Daily Journal of Commerce*, August, 1871.
21. "The Story of an Early Day Kansan," in *The Club Member* (Topeka), May, 1909, p. 10.
22. Adapted from Inman, *Old Santa Fe Trail*, 205-206.
23. Ellsworth *Reporter*, January 11, 1871.
24. *Ford County Globe*, August 5, 1879.
25. Cook, *The Border and the Buffalo*, 292.

Bibliography

Andreas, A. T. *History of the State of Kansas*. Illustrated. Chicago, A. T. Andreas.

Bentley, O. H. Editor. *History of Wichita and Sedgwick County, Kansas*. Chicago, C. F. Cooper & Co., 2 Vols.

Blackmar, Frank W. Editor. *Kansas; a Cyclopedia of State History*. In two volumes. Chicago, Standard Publishing Co.

Blanchard, Leola Howard. *Conquest of Southwest Kansas*. Wichita, The Wichita Eagle Press.

Bowles, Samuel. *Across the Continent;* a Summer's Journey to the Rocky Mountains, the Mormons, and the Pacific States, with Speaker Colfax. Springfield, Mass., Samuel Bowles & Co.; New York, Hurd & Houghton.

Bradley, Glenn Danford. *The Story of the Pony Express;* an Account of the Most Remarkable Mail Service Ever in Existence, and Its Place in History. Chicago, A. C. McClurg & Co.

Chapman, Arthur. *The Pony Express;* the Record of a Romantic Adventure in Business. New York and London, G. P. Putnam's Sons.

205

Cody, Mrs. Louisa (Frederici). *Memories of Buffalo Bill,* by His Wife. New York, London, D. Appleton and Co.

Cody, William Frederick. *An Autobiography of Buffalo Bill* (Colonel W. F. Cody). New York, Cosmopolitan Book Corporation.

Cook, John R. *The Border and the Buffalo;* an Untold Story of the Southwest Plains. Topeka, Kansas, Monotyped and Printed by Crane and Co.

Connelley, William Elsey. *Wild Bill and His Era;* the Life and Adventures of James Butler Hickok. New York, Press of the Pioneers.

Foy, Eddie, *pseud.,* and Harlow, Alvin F. *Clowning Through Life,* by Eddie Foy (pseud. of Edward Fitzgerald), and Alvin F. Harlow. New York, E. P. Dutton & Company.

Greeley, Horace. *An Overland Journey* from New York to San Francisco in the Summer of 1859. New York, C. M. Saxton, Barker & Co.; San Francisco, H. H. Bancroft & Co.

Greene, Max. *The Kanzas Region:* Forest, Prairie, Desert, Mountain, Vale, and River. New York, Fowler and Wells, Publishers.

Hardin, John Wesley. *Life of John Wesley Hardin* Written by Himself and Published from Original Manuscript in 1896 by Smith & Moore. Republished, 1925, with Additions by Frontier Times. Bandera, Texas, Frontier Times, 1925.

Henry, Stuart. *Conquering Our Great American Plains.* New York, E. P. Dutton & Co., Inc.

Hunter, John Marvin, Compiler and Editor. *The Trail Drivers of Texas.* 2nd ed. Rev. (Two volumes in one). Nashville, Tenn., Cokesbury Press.

Inman, Col. Henry. *The Old Santa Fe Trail;* the Story of a Great Highway. Topeka Crane & Co.

Kansas State Historical Society. *Collections.* Volumes IX, X, and XVII. Topeka, State Printer, 1906-1928. Five articles in these volumes have been used as follows:

Bernard, William R. Westport and the Santa Fe Trade, Vol. IX, p. 552-565.

Dick, Everett. The Long Drive, Vol. XVII, p. 27-97.

Hadley, James Albert and Beeson, Chalkley, M. A Royal Buffalo Hunt, Vol. X, p. 564-580.

Moore, Ely. A Buffalo Hunt with the Miamis in 1854, Vol. X, p. 402-409.

Two City Marshals; Thomas James Smith, of Abilene, Vol. IX, p. 526-532.

Keim, De B. Randolph. *Sheridan's Troopers on the Border:* A Winter Campaign on the Plains. Philadelphia, Claxton, Remson & Haffelfinger.

Majors, Alexander. *Seventy Years on the Frontier.* Alexander Majors' Memoirs of a Lifetime on the Border. Chicago, Rand McNally & Co.

McCoy, Joseph G. *Historic Sketches of the Cattle Trade of the West and Southwest.* Kansas City, Mo., Ramsey, Millett & Hudson, 1874. Reprinted, Washington, D. C., The Rare Book Shop, 1932.

Nimmo, Joseph. *Report in Regard to the Range and Ranch Cattle Traffic in the Western States,* made to the Secretary of the Treasury, February, 1885. (U.S. 48th Congress, 2nd Session. House Executive Documents, Vol. 29, No. 267).

Richardson, Albert D. *Beyond the Mississippi.* From the Great River to the Great Ocean. Life and Adventure on the Prairies, Mountains, and Pacific Coast. Hartford, Conn., American Publishing Co.; Philadelphia, Cincinnati, Davenport, Atlanta, National Publishing Co.; New York, Bliss & Co.; San Francisco, H. H. Bancroft & Co.

Root, Frank A. and Connelley, William Elsey. *The Overland Stage to California.* Published by the authors. Topeka, Kansas.

Sheridan, Philip Henry. *Report of Major General P. H. Sheridan.* (In U.S. War Department. Report of the Secretary of War, 1868-69. Vol. I. Washington, Gov't. Print. (Serial No. 1367).

Siringo, Charles A. *A Lone Star Cowboy.* Cleveland, The Arthur H. Clark Co.

Walton, W. M. *Life and Adventures of Ben Thompson* (Republished in Frontier Times. Bandera, Texas, vol. 3, No. 10 to vol. 4, No. 3. July-December, 1926). First Published in 1884.

Webb, William Edward. *Buffalo Land;* an Authentic Account of the Discoveries, Adventures, and Mishaps of a Scientific and Sporting Party in the Wild West. Cincinnati and Chicago, E. Hannaford & Co.; Boston, J. Friday & Co.; San Francisco, A. L. Bancroft & Co.

Wetmore, Helen Cody. *Last of the Great Scouts;* the Life Story of Col. William F. Cody "Buffalo Bill." As told by His Sister, Helen Cody Wetmore. Chicago and Duluth, The Duluth Press Publishing Co.

Wright, Robert Marr. *Dodge City, the Cowboy Capital,* and the Great Southwest in the Days of the Wild Indian, the Buffalo, the Cowboy, Dance Halls, Gambling Halls, and Bad Men. Wichita, Kans., Wichita Eagle Press.

Young, Charles Edward. *Dangers of the Trail in* 1865; a Narrative of Actual Events. Geneva, N. Y. Press of W. F. Humphrey.

Index

Abilene, Kansas, 53-54, 60, 66, 67, 70-92

Abilene *Chronicle*, 55, 81, 89

Alexis, Grand Duke, 182-184

Allen, Dr. E. B., 136

Allen, H. C., 189

Anderson, Hugh, 87, 132-138

Anderson, James H. (Pop), 138

Anderson, William, 147

Arapaho Indians, 19, 20, 39

Arkansas River, 4, 13, 32, 34, 48-49, 53, 54, 59, 63

Atchison, Kansas, 5, 7, 9, 23, 28

Atchison, Topeka and Santa Fe Railroad, 84, 126, 144

Aubrey, François Xavier, 29-34

Auer, David, 162

Bailey, William, 131-132

Baker, Harry, 197

Baldwin, Lieutenant, 191

Barber, E., 79, 81

Bardsley, Sheriff, 162-163

Baumann, Charles, 138, 140

Baxter Springs, Kansas, 54

Beard, John (Red), 145, 146, 147

Beaver Creek, 177

Beebe, Jerome, 94, 95, 99, 105, 106, 113

Behrens, John, 149, 154

Bent, Bill, 17

Bentley, S. J., 127

Berkley, Johnny, 193

Bernard, Joe, 193-194

Bessie, Policeman, 118

Bideno (Mexican herder), 86-87, 133

Big Blue River, 4

Big Creek, 191, 194

Big Elk, Chief, 172-174

"Big Hank," 77

Bluff, Kansas, 87

Bond, "Brick," 170

Boone, Attorney General, 121

Border and the Buffalo, The (Cook), 197

Boston, Mrs. Anna Campbell, 192

Botts, Samuel, 151, 154

Boudinot, L., 84

Bowles, Samuel, 21

Bowman, Cy, 136

Boyd, Dr. Gaston, 136, 140

Brauham, John S., 101

Brennan, Joseph, 95, 102, 103, 105

Brennan, Molly, 108

Brewster, General, 15-19

Brinkman, G. S., 84, 85

Brooks, William, 138-139, 141

Brookville, Kansas, 117

Bross, William, 21

Brown, H. C., 73, 76

Brown, J. C. (Charlie), 115, 116, 117, 118, 161

Brown, Saul, 115

Brunner, Henry, 131, 140-141, 142

"Buffalo Hunter, The" (song), 197

Buffalo Land (Webb), 194

Buffaloes, 10, 58, 167-198

Bullwhackers, 50-51

Burdett, James, 121

Burns, Harry, 197

Burris, Samuel, 151

Burroughs, S. A., 84

Buskirk, Frank, 165

Butterfield, David, 9, 70

Butterfield Overland Dispatch, 9-10, 15-16

Caches, The, 48-49
Cahn, James, 159-160
Cahn, Joseph, 159
Cain, Neil, 98, 103, 108, 112, 113, 119, 120
Cairns, James, 149
Caldwell, Kansas, 54
Calhoun, Mr., 15
Callahan, Jack, 192
Campbell, Mr. and Mrs. Perry, 192
Campbell, William P., 151
Canadian River, 54
Carpenter, A. L., 13
Carpenter, Samuel, 84
Carson, Kit, 84, 137
Carson, Thomas, 84-85, 87, 137
Case, A. H., 124, 125
Cattle, 53-68
Cattle trails, 53-68
  high water and, 62-64
  Indian attacks and, 58, 64-65
  outlaws and, 65-66
  stampedes, 57, 60, 61-62, 66
Cattlemen, 53-68
  farmers versus, 66-68
Chambers, Alice, 157
Cherry Creek, 9
Cheyenne Indians, 14, 19, 20, 39, 186-188
Chisholm, Jesse, 54
Chisholm Trail, 54, 71
Chorn, William, 86, 133
Cimarron, Kansas, 4
Clarkson Brothers, 180-182
Clay Center, Kansas, 80
Clements boys, 86
Coaches, see Stage coaches
Cody, William F. (Buffalo Bill), 29, 30, 95, 167-168, 177-180, 182, 183, 184
Coe, Phil, 83, 84, 86, 89, 90, 91
Coke, Governor, 121
Cole, Amos, 182-183
Comstock, William, 178-180
Colfax, Schuyler, 21, 29
Colorado, 7
Cook, John R., 197

Corwin, Sheriff, 119, 121
Cotton, Bud, 91
Council Grove, Kansas, 3, 39-41
Council Springs, Kansas, 167
Cow Creek, 13
Cow towns, Kansas, 69-166
Cowboys, 53, 55-56, 60, 61, 62, 73, 74, 77, 81, 97, 131
Cowskin Creek, 59
Cox, William M., 54, 97
Cox's Trail, 54, 97
Cramer, Joseph, 79, 81
Crawford, Ed, 110, 112, 113, 118
Creek Indians, 65
Cunningham, Ernest, 115
Custer, George A., 182

Dallas Commercial, 122
Dalton, James, 165
Davis, Jackson, 146
Davis, Theodore R., 15, 17
Davis, Willard, 125
Deger, Larry E., 156-157
Delaney, Arthur, see McCluskie, Mike
DeLong, John, 100-101, 110, 116
Denver (gambler), 157
Denver, Colorado, 4, 5, 7, 8, 9, 28, 29
Dibb, William, 149
Dodge City, Kansas, 55, 68, 82, 119, 126, 139, 145, 155-166, 169
Dodge City Times, 158, 197
Doheney, E. L., 144
Donhoe, J. A., 32
Duck, W. M., 107
Durfey, Jeff, 176

Earle, E. O., 190
Earp, Wyatt, 95, 151
Egan, James, 190
Eicholtz, W. H., 84
Ellsworth, Kansas, 54, 55, 67-68, 70-71, 75, 82-83, 92-126, 183
Ellsworth Cattle Trail, see Cox's Trail
Ellsworth County Farmers Protective Society, 68
Ellsworth Reporter, 95, 96, 100, 104, 113, 125, 126, 183
Emigrant trains, see Wagon trains

Emmerson, Mr., 162-164
Enox, Frank, 119, 120
Evans, R. W., 156

Fancher, Washburne, 73
Farmers, cattlemen versus, 66-68
Finlaw, William, 106
Fitzpatrick, Pat, 141-142
Flint, Edward R., 28
Folsom, California, 37
Forbes, Archibald, 183
Ford County Globe, 156, 158, 197
Forsyth, George A., 182
Forsyth, James W., 182
Fort Dodge, 20
Fort Zarah, 167
Fowler, J. L., 190
Foy, Eddie, 82, 155
Fraker, D. H., 113
Franklin, Annie, 147
Freebourn, Richard, 116
Freight trains, *see* Wagon trains
Frey, Johnnie, 35-37

Gainsford, James, 80, 84, 85, 88
Garden City, Kansas, 68
Garrett, William, 133, 135, 136
George, M. B., 72, 94
Gessler, S., 148
Gill, Robert, 125, 126
Gladdon, George, 120
Goddard Brothers, 177
Good, John, 112, 116, 117
Good, Mat, 108
Gore, J. W., 72, 94, 99, 110
Gore, Louisa, 72, 94
Great Bend, Kansas, 88
Greeley, Horace, 23-26, 28, 38
Gunn, James, 165

Hall, Jim, 187
Halliday, George, 141-142
Hamill, Dave, 142
Hamilton, Samuel, 121, 123
Hammer, Captain, 13
Hardin, Wes, 73, 86, 133
Hardships, encountered along wagon
    trails, 8-9, 10, 11-23, 39
Harper's Weekly, 15

Hasbrouck, Lawrence, 15, 17
Hays, Kansas, 51, 71, 75, 84, 156, 162,
    177, 180, 181, 186-188, 194
Hays *Sentinel*, 158
Hazel, Jessie, 89
Henry, Dutch, 160-164
Henry, Theodore C., 72, 73
Hersey, Tim, 70, 73
Hersey, Mrs. Tim, 70
Hickok, J. B. (Wild Bill), 72, 84, 85-
    86, 88-92, 95, 137
Hicks, Dan, 139-141
Higley, Brewster, 198
Hogue, Ed O., 100, 101, 109, 110, 112-
    113, 118-119
Holladay, Ben, 5, 10, 26-28, 70
Holladay, Mrs. Ben, 26-27
Hollenberg, Kansas, 36
"Home on the Range, A" (song),
    198
Hooker, J. F., 149
Hope, James G., 149, 153
Horseback rides, record, 29-38
Hunter, R. D., 96

Independence, Missouri, 3, 4, 5, 28,
    29, 30, 31, 33, 38
Indian Territory, 53, 54, 55, 64
Indianola, Kansas, 7
Indians, *See also* names of tribes, 3,
    6
    buffalo hunting with, 170-176
    depredations by, 7, 9, 10, 11-20, 21,
        41, 42-45, 49-50, 58, 64-65, 93, 194
Inman, Henry, 102, 168, 170, 184
Iowa City, Iowa, 42
Irvin, Mr., 131

Jenkins, Lieutenant, 13
Jennison, Charley, 146
Jewett, E. B., 150, 153
John, Sam, 108, 161
Johnston, J. R. (Jack), 141, 142
Jones, Russell, and Company (Leav-
    enworth), 7
Jordan, Kirk, 139
Junction City, Kansas, 7, 54, 80, 81
Junction City *Union*, 89, 100

Kansas Pacific Railroad, 53, 55, 70-71,

115, 167, 169, 172, 177, 178, 184-185, 193, 194
Kansas River, 8
Karatofsky, Jac. (Jake), 71, 89, 147
Kaw River, 4, 7
Kearnes, Henry, 133, 136
Keim, De B. Randolph, 167, 168, 184-185, 191
Kelley, James H., 156, 159
Kelly, John, 94, 100, 110, 116
Kelly, Peter, 13-14
Kennekuk, Kansas, 5, 36
Krum, E. P., 128
Kuney, C. C., 80

La-Flesche, Frank, 173, 174
Ladder Creek, 181
Langford, W. A., 105
Larkin, Arthur, 94, 95
Lawrence, Kansas, 23-24
Leavenworth, Kansas, 7, 8, 22, 23, 24, 124, 125
Leavenworth and Pike's Peak Express, 7-8, 23, 24, 28
Leavenworth Times, 123
Lebold, C. H., 73
Lee, Patrick, 136
Lentz, Nick, 94, 100, 103, 104, 105, 107
Leverett, Sergeant, 121
Ligon, David, 122
Little Blue River, 36, 66
Little Raven, Chief, 25
Lloyd, Ira E., 125
Lovett, Harry, 128, 141
Lowe, Joseph (Rowdy Joe), 95, 145-146, 147
Lowe, Kate, 145

Mabry, Seth, 96, 104, 109
Majors, Alexander, 44, 51
Manhattan, Kansas, 24
Marion, Kansas, 65, 148
Martin, Jim, 133, 135, 136
Martin, William, 65, 148-149, 152
Martinez, Jesus M., 49-50
Marston, J. D., 191
Marysville, Kansas, 5, 36
Massey, P. H., 149
Masterson, Bat, 82

Masterson, Ed, 164
Masterson, Sheriff, 163
Masterson, W. B., 166
McCluskie, Mike, 131-136
McConnell, Andrew, 78-80
McCoy, Joseph G., 53, 67, 71, 72, 73, 84, 85, 129
McDonald, James H., 76, 79, 80, 84, 85, 88
McGee, Frank, 112
McGlue, Luke, 165, 166
McGrath, Thomas, 153-154
McMichael, Captain, 19
Meagher, John, 149
Meagher, Michael, 149
Meredith, Doctor, 165-166
Miami Indians, 170-171
Miles, Moses, 79, 80
Milford, Kansas, 80
Miller, James, 99, 109, 110-111, 115, 116
Millett, Alonzo, 96
Millett, Eugene, 104
Mirages, 48
Missouri Commonwealth, 4
Missouri River, 6, 34, 35, 36
Mohler, J. D., 125
Monk, Hank, 25-26
Montgomery, John, 100, 102, 104, 108
Monument Station, 41
Moon, Sheriff, 122, 123
Moore, Ely, 170
Morco, John (Happy Jack), 101-107, 109, 110, 113, 116-117
Morco, Mrs. John, 117-118
Mormon Grove, 42
Mormons, 42
Morphy, W. N., 156, 189
Muse, R. W. P., 142
Musgrove, Captain, 19
Myers, J. J., 96

Nagle, Bill, 107
Nebraska, 4, 5, 55
New, Jake, 94, 103, 104, 107
New York Tribune, 23, 24, 169
Newton, Kansas, 54, 84, 87, 88, 126-143
Newton and Southwestern Railroad, 145

Nimmo, Joseph, 55
Ninnescah River, 59
Noel, J. W., 118
Norton, John W. (Brocky Jack),
    100, 104, 105, 107, 110-111

O'Fallen's, Nebraska, 190
Okmulkee route, 54, 65
Old Shawnee Trail, 54
Oldham, Jonathan, 23
Olive, J. P., 99
Omaha Indians, 172-176
Oregon Trail, 3, 4
Osawatomie, Kansas, 23
Osborn, Governor, 119
Osborne, Vincent B., 83, 101, 102,
    109
Otero, Miguel, 15
Otero and Sellar (freighters), 51
Otis, George K., 21
Outlaws, 65-66
Overland Stage Line, 4, 5, 7, 8, 11,
    21, 23, 25, 28-29
Overstreet, Rev. R. M., 130

Palmer, Innis N., 182
Palmer, Lizzy, 118
Parks, Daniel, 149
Pawnee Indians, 42-43
Peak, Justice, 123
Pendleton, Phil, 124, 125
Perrin, Mr., 16, 17
Peryman, W. S., and Company, 96
Peters, Judge, 164
Philip, William D., 180
Pierce, Abel H., 97
Pierce, Cad, 98, 103, 104, 107, 108,
    109, 112-113, 114, 116, 118
Placerville, California, 5, 6, 26, 28, 37
Platte River, 4, 5, 7, 8, 22, 29, 36, 37
Pleasures, enjoyed by stage-coach
    passengers, 10-11
Pond Creek, 41
Pony Express, 29, 35-38
Prentice, Thaddeus, 23

Railroads, see also names of rail-
    roads, 4, 35, 51, 53
Rambling Jim, 197
Ramsey (Texan), 150

Ramsey, Alexander, 161
Red River, 54, 60
Republican River, 7, 80, 182
Richardson, Albert D., 21, 24, 169
Rides, record horseback, 29-38
Robbins, Mr., 76
Robinson, Major, 191-192
Robinson, Sergeant, 122
Rodgers, Jim, 87
Rodman, Sheriff, 80
Roff, Harry, 37
Rothenburg, Ike, 159
Russell, Majors and Waddell, 38-39,
    44, 51
Russell, W. A., 127
Russell, William H., 35
Ryan, Dennis, 191
Ryan, John, 79

Sacramento, California, 6, 36, 37
Sacramento River, 36, 37
Sage, Rufus B., 42-43
St. Johns, E., 191
St. Joseph, Missouri, 6, 35, 37-38
St. Louis, Missouri, 4, 30, 33
St. Louis Daily Union, 33
Salina, Kansas, 114-115, 116, 117, 123
Saline County Journal, 58, 115
Salt Lake City, Utah, 6, 37
San Francisco, California, 35, 36, 37
Santa Fe, New Mexico, 4, 5, 28, 29,
    30, 31, 32, 33, 48
Santa Fe Herald, 33
Santa Fe Railroad, see Atchison,
    Topeka and Santa Fe Railroad
Santa Fe Republican, 32
Santa Fe Trail, 3-4, 13, 20, 30, 38, 39,
    40
    treasure legend of the, 49-50
Saunders, Charley, 150
Schermerhorn, Ed, 183
Schmitt, Andrew, 100, 110
Seitz, George, 95, 99, 105
Seneca, Kansas, 36, 37
Seward, Charles, 118
Shane, James B., 73
Shaw, Bob, 164-165
Shea, John, 79
Sheran, Thomas, 73, 84
Sheridan, Philip H., 30, 182

Sherman, Tom, 157
Sherman, William T., 167, 168
Sierra Nevada Mountains, 25
Sioux Indians, 39
Siringo, Charley, 97
Smith, Judge, 120
Smith, Thomas J., 75-80, 85
Smith, William, 149, 150, 152, 153
Smith County Pioneer, 198
Smoky Hill River, 8
Smoky Hill Route, 8, 9, 20, 28, 39
Snakes, 47-48
Snyder, Sam, 159
Solomon River, 7, 163, 173, 177
Songs of the range, 197-198
Sparks, J. C., 119-123
Stage coaches, 4-9
    hardships encountered by passengers, 8-9, 10, 11-23
    pleasures enjoyed by passengers, 10-11
    record trips made by, 28-29
Stage lines, 4-10
Stampedes, 57, 60, 61-62, 66
Stebbins, H. D., 99-100
Stein, Lenas, 183, 184
Sterling, John, 98, 103, 104, 107, 109
Sternberg, William, 172
Stevens, Deputy Sheriff, 118, 161
Stewart, Eb, 119, 120
Storms, 21-23, 192-193
Strangham (Stawhan), Samuel, 84
Stroud, Captain, 17
Sweet, Jim, 145

Tamblyn, Colonel, 16
Tegener, Judge, 120, 121
Texas (Negro), 157
Texas Dick, 164-165
Thompson, Ben, 82-84, 86, 88-90, 91, 95, 98, 102-112, 114-115, 120, 121, 122, 124, 126, 148
Thompson, Billy, 82, 83, 95, 98, 101-111, 119-126
Thompson, C. H., 70
Thompson, Jim, 155
Thompson Creek, 192
Todd, Charley, 193
Topeka, Kansas, 4
Topeka *Commonwealth*, 96, 115

Towns, Kansas cow, 69-166
Trail-driving, 53-68
Trails
    cattle, 53-68
    wagon, 3-52
Trains, wagon, 38-47
Treasure, buried, 49-50
Tucker, S. M., 151-152
Turner, Judge, 121
Tuttle, Perry, 128, 133, 134, 136, 138

Union Pacific Railroad, 75, 168

Vansicle, Mr., 193

Wagon trails, 3-52
    hardships encountered along, 8-9, 10, 11-23, 39
    Indian attacks, 7, 9, 10, 11-20, 31, 41, 42-45, 49-50
    mirages and, 48
    pleasures enjoyed on, 10-11
    snakes and, 47-48
    storms, 21-23
Wagon trains, 38-47
Wakarusa Creek, 23
Walton, W. M., 82, 107, 112
Waters, Mose, 156
Weakly, Sheriff, 162
Webb, W. E., 185-186, 188, 194
Webster, A. B., 156
Weightman, R. H., 33-34
West Shawnee Trail, 54
Whipple, Doctor, 17, 18
White Wolf, Chief, 186-188
Whitney, Chauncey B., 82, 100, 102, 104-108, 111-112, 119, 120, 121, 123, 126
Wichita, Kansas, 53, 54, 59, 143-154
Wichita *Eagle*, 150
"Wild Huntress," 194-197
Wilkerson, Jim, 133, 136
Williams, George H., 115
Williams, Mike, 90, 91
Wilson, William, *see* Bailey, William
Wyandote Indians, 41
Wyoming Frank, 77-78

Zaun, Charles, 162